James Watson

Jedburgh Abbey : historical and descriptive

James Watson

Jedburgh Abbey : historical and descriptive

ISBN/EAN: 9783742855503

Manufactured in Europe, USA, Canada, Australia, Japa

Cover: Foto ©Andreas Hilbeck / pixelio.de

Manufactured and distributed by brebook publishing software (www.brebook.com)

James Watson

Jedburgh Abbey : historical and descriptive

JEDBURGH ABBEY FROM SOUTH-EAST

JEDBURGH ABBEY:

HISTORICAL AND DESCRIPTIVE

ALSO

THE ABBEYS OF TEVIOTDALE

AS SHOWING THE DEVELOPMENT OF GOTHIC
ARCHITECTURE

BY

JAMES WATSON

ASSOCIATE MEMBER OF THE BERWICKSHIRE NATURALISTS' CLUB
AUTHOR OF THE "GUIDE TO JEDBURGH," ETC.

SECOND EDITION, REVISED AND GREATLY ENLARGED

"There it stands,
And there will stand, till the slow tooth of Time
Nibble it all away."—THOMAS AIRD.
"Thou mayst behold,
Outside and inside both, pillars and roofs,
Carved work, the hand of famed artificers."—MILTON.

EDINBURGH: DAVID DOUGLAS
1894

[*All rights reserved.*]

TO THE

Most Honourable Schomberg Henry Kerr,

NINTH MARQUESS OF LOTHIAN, K.T., P.C., ETC.,

A NOBLEMAN WHOSE PUBLIC SERVICES AND PRIVATE WORTH HAVE

ENDEARED HIM TO HIS COUNTRYMEN, AND

TO WHOM THEY OWE THE PRESERVATIVE RESTORATION

OF JEDBURGH ABBEY,

THIS WORK IS,

BY THE KIND PERMISSION OF HIS LORDSHIP,

RESPECTFULLY DEDICATED

BY THE AUTHOR.

PREFACE TO THE FIRST EDITION.

To narrate concisely whatever is at present known of the history of Jedburgh Abbey and its inmates, to ascertain the successive stages of its architectural growth, to trace its decay, and to describe its ruins, is the purpose of the following pages.

Compared with the sister establishments of Melrose, Kelso, and Dryburgh, the materials for a history of Jedburgh Abbey are peculiarly scanty. The chartularies of the three first-named abbeys are still extant, but everything that the monks of Jedburgh may have recorded, whether relating to the private affairs of their convent, the rich domains attached to it, or the many public events in which it was concerned, has unfortunately perished. This being the case, the facts necessary for a history of this monastery had to be gathered from a great variety of sources, and were therefore of a disconnected character. The first important contribution was from the pen of the Rev. James Morton, B.D., the result of whose indefatigable labours is contained in his valuable and well-known work, *The Monastic Annals of Teviotdale*, which appeared in 1832; and it may safely be said that the subject stands very much where he left it, little of importance having been added since his time.

Every effort has been made to render the historical portion of the present work as complete as circumstances would permit, and much valuable information has been procured from unpublished records, including many in the General Register House, Edinburgh, private charters, and the Records of the Presbytery, Heritors, and

PREFACE TO THE FIRST EDITION.

To narrate concisely whatever is at present known of the history of Jedburgh Abbey and its inmates, to ascertain the successive stages of its architectural growth, to trace its decay, and to describe its ruins, is the purpose of the following pages.

Compared with the sister establishments of Melrose, Kelso, and Dryburgh, the materials for a history of Jedburgh Abbey are peculiarly scanty. The chartularies of the three first-named abbeys are still extant, but everything that the monks of Jedburgh may have recorded, whether relating to the private affairs of their convent, the rich domains attached to it, or the many public events in which it was concerned, has unfortunately perished. This being the case, the facts necessary for a history of this monastery had to be gathered from a great variety of sources, and were therefore of a disconnected character. The first important contribution was from the pen of the Rev. James Morton, B.D., the result of whose indefatigable labours is contained in his valuable and well-known work, *The Monastic Annals of Teviotdale*, which appeared in 1832; and it may safely be said that the subject stands very much where he left it, little of importance having been added since his time.

Every effort has been made to render the historical portion of the present work as complete as circumstances would permit, and much valuable information has been procured from unpublished records, including many in the General Register House, Edinburgh, private charters, and the Records of the Presbytery, Heritors, and

Town Council of Jedburgh. The statements of previous writers have been carefully tested, and exception has been taken to these only where they were at variance with documentary evidence. An attempt is here made for the first time to give a connected account of the various changes of ownership of the abbey lands from the Reformation to their finally becoming, by Crown charter, the property of the Lothian family. The task is not without difficulty, as perplexities and apparent contradictions occur, which it is not easy altogether to remove or to reconcile; but the account here presented may be accepted as substantially accurate so far as it goes, and may perhaps lighten the labours of other investigators. While treating on this part of the subject I have gladly availed myself of certain notes with which I was favoured by William Fraser, Esq., S.S.C., Edinburgh.

The architectural description will be found to be much more minute than any hitherto given; and it may be stated that while fixing the approximate dates of the various portions of the ruins, not only have the architectural styles been considered, but also the social condition of the district at the different times.

In acknowledging the assistance and encouragement received from several gentlemen in the preparation of this work, I have much pleasure in expressing my obligations to David Laing, Esq., Signet Library, Edinburgh, whose name has so long been connected with the elucidation of the early history and literature of Scotland, and to whom I am indebted also for the two old views of the abbey, 1775 and 1777.

The gentleman to whom I have been most largely indebted, however, is Archibald Carlyle Mounsey, Esq., Queen Mary's House,

Jedburgh, and I shall ever gratefully remember the very valuable services rendered by him. Not only did he in the most handsome manner place at my disposal a large collection of MSS., and a number of rare books from his own library, many of the former being original charters and others copied from our national archives, but he also most unreservedly gave me the advantage of his assistance in dealing with difficulties, and of his advice generally.

I have also much pleasure in acknowledging the facilities afforded by Thomas Dickson, Esq., H.M. General Register House, for consulting various documents under his charge.

JAMES WATSON.

JEDBURGH, 18*th June* 1877.

PREFACE TO THE SECOND EDITION.

The first edition of this work, which has long been out of print, was well received both by the press and the public, and in preparing the present edition no pains have been spared to make it even more worthy of acceptance. Though it was stated in the former preface that the chartulary of Jedburgh Abbey had perished, there were those who still fondly cherished the hope that it might be discovered; but all such hope may be abandoned, as it is now proved, on incontrovertible evidence, that the charters and muniments of this religious house were lost and destroyed by war and other fortuitous causes. This being the case, all chances are gone of ever having a consecutive and continuous history of the Abbey such as might otherwise have been. However, a considerable amount of additional historical information has been gleaned from different quarters and embodied here, much of it now published for the first time. Every effort has been made to ensure accuracy, and reference is made to the sources whence most of the information has been derived.

In the present edition several new features have been introduced, including the Temporality and Spirituality of the Abbey, an Account of the Notable Persons Buried in the Abbey, and several Charters relative to the Monastery. A few names have been added to our previous List of Abbots, which was by far the fullest and most accurate ever before published, and the collection of Masons' Marks has also been considerably added to.

The number of illustrations has been increased from four to fifteen, including an interesting plan drawn in 1760. The modern views of the Abbey give a fair idea of its architecture, while the old views will be found to be of value to the antiquary. The sketch of the ancient cross which faces page 128, and which has not been previously figured, I owe to the kindness of Mr Alexander Galletly, of the Museum of Science and Art, Edinburgh.

To Dr Hardie, the indefatigable Secretary of the Berwickshire Naturalists' Club, and to Mr W. B. Cook, Stirling, who has devoted much time to antiquarian research, I am indebted for some valuable notes. I have also pleasure in again acknowledging my obligations to my old and valued friend, Mr A. C. Mounsey, Jedburgh, for his learned assistance, more especially in deciphering old documents, which could only have been done by an expert. To these and other gentlemen who have given me assistance in any way I wish to make due acknowledgment.

Considering the growing interest in our grand ecclesiastical ruins, the account of the Abbeys of Teviotdale at the end of this book will, I trust, be thought a not unfitting conclusion to a work devoted to one of the most important of the group. The sketch originally appeared as two articles in the *Scotsman* newspaper some years ago, and not a few people have expressed a wish to see it in a more accessible form.

JAMES WATSON.

JEDBURGH, 27th October 1893.

CONTENTS.

	PAGE
INTRODUCTORY, .	1
THE FIRST CHURCH AT JEDBURGH, .	7
THE MONASTERY AS FOUNDED BY DAVID,	11
ERECTION OF NAVE AND EXTENSION OF CHOIR,	15
EVENTS BETWEEN 1220 AND 1285,	22
A ROYAL MARRIAGE IN THE ABBEY,	28
THE EFFECTS OF THE WAR OF INDEPENDENCE ON THE ABBEY,	32
REBUILDING OF THE NORTH TRANSEPT, CHOIR CHAPEL, AND TOWER,	39
FURTHER VICISSITUDES: BURNING OF THE ABBEY BY THE ENGLISH,	48
EVENTS BETWEEN 1500 AND 1560,	51
THE REFORMATION: SUPPRESSION OF THE MONASTERY,	55
THE ALTARAGES IN THE ABBEY,	67
THE SEAL OF THE CHAPTER OF JEDBURGH,	70
SUPERIORS OF THE MONASTERY,	72
THE REFORMED CHURCH IN THE ABBEY, .	81
MINISTERS OF THE REFORMED CHURCH IN THE ABBEY, .	105
REMOVAL OF THE CHURCH FROM THE ABBEY, .	112
THE DOUBLE ROOF-MARKS ON THE ABBEY,	118
MASONS' MARKS ON THE ABBEY,	122

CONTENTS.

	PAGE
MEASUREMENTS OF THE ABBEY CHURCH, .	125
SCULPTURED STONES IN THE ABBEY,	127
NOTABLE PERSONS BURIED IN THE ABBEY,	130
POSSESSIONS AND REVENUES OF THE ABBEY,	146
RENT ROLL OF THE ABBEY,	151
SPIRITUALITY OF THE ABBEY, .	155
CHARTERS RELATIVE TO JEDBURGH ABBEY,	159
THE ABBEYS OF TEVIOTDALE, AS SHOWING THE DEVELOPMENT OF GOTHIC ARCHITECTURE,	169

LIST OF ILLUSTRATIONS.

JEDBURGH ABBEY FROM THE SOUTH-EAST,		*facing title-page*	
Do.	NORMAN ARCHES IN CHOIR,	*facing page*	12
Do.	ARCHES IN NAVE FROM THE NORTH-WEST,	,,	16
Do.	SOUTH DOORWAY,	,,	18
Do.	WEST DOORWAY,	,,	19
Do.	FROM THE NORTH IN 1877,	,,	41
Do.	FROM THE NORTH-EAST IN 1775,	,,	93
PLAN OF ABBEY KIRK OF JEDBURGH, WITH THE MANSE, OFFICES, HOUSE, GARDEN, &c., IN 1760, .		,,	95
JEDBURGH ABBEY FROM THE NORTH IN 1777,		,,	98
ANTIQUE KEY FOUND IN THE ABBEY,		,,	114
JEDBURGH ABBEY FROM THE SOUTH-WEST IN 1790,		,,	115
MASONS' MARKS ON JEDBURGH ABBEY,		,,	124
ANGLO CROSS IN JEDBURGH ABBEY,		,,	127
ANCIENT CROSS, NOW FORMING A LINTEL IN JEDBURGH ABBEY, .		,,	128
ROMAN INSCRIPTION IN JEDBURGH ABBEY,		*page*	128

INTRODUCTORY.

MONACHISM, as is well known, had its origin in the East at a very early period. The Essenes and other Jewish fraternities were ascetics; but it was not until the second century of our era that any of the Christians betook themselves to a life of solitude, and that more by accident than choice. In consequence of the barbarous persecution instituted by the Roman emperor Decius against those who professed to be followers of the meek and lowly Jesus, multitudes of Christians fled from their homes, among whom was Paul, a native of Thebes, who travelled far into the desert and took up his abode in a cave in one of the mountains. Paul, who was a noble and learned youth, was the first Christian hermit. In that lonely spot he lived ninety years, with the cave as his only shelter, the fruit of the palm-tree his only food, the leaves of the palm-tree his only raiment, and the water of the fountain his only drink. His time was spent in meditation and prayer, and he died, it is said, in the 130th year of his age. Immediately before that event occurred he was visited by St Anthony, who had lived in a similar way in a different part of the country. The visitor arrived just in time to witness Paul's immortal part, "luminous and shining," ascend towards heaven, amidst a host of angels and apostles, while his body was in the attitude of prayer. At least so says the legend.

St Anthony, who in his solitary home had many wrestlings with the Evil One, was believed to have the power of working miracles, and his fame was such that numbers of people flocked to him, not only to receive spiritual advice, but also to be cured of bodily or mental disease. He brought together a large number of hermits, who made dwellings near each other—forming a sort of village, or *laura*, as it was called—and they combined together in prayer and in procuring the necessaries of life. They became what are known as cenobites, living in common and obeying St Anthony as their superior, being thus distinguished from anchorites or eremites, who lived alone and owned no superior. St Anthony, who is regarded as the founder of monachism, and of whom many wonderful stories are told, died on Mount Coltzim, on the borders of the Red Sea, when 104 years old.

One of his disciples, named Pachomius, whom Dr Zimmerman considered to be incomparably more sensible and a far greater man than his master, founded the first regular cloister about 325. This was at Tabenna, a village on an island of the Nile. He had only fourteen monks under him at that place, but before he died there were many thousands living under his rule. They had to work at various kinds of handicrafts, the principal of which was the making of mats. He also founded a nunnery at Tabenna, and those who entered it were required to cut off their hair and cover their faces with the sacred veil. The rage for the monastic life became so great that in Egypt alone in 346—the year of the death of Pachomius—no fewer than 76,000 men and 27,000 women are said to have embraced it. "All the girls in the world," says Zimmerman, "whom stupidity, superstition, and inhuman madness have locked up in cloisters, that they may there abandon and despise the world, do violence to nature, stifle their best affections, and have their most innocent and sweetest emotions condemned by a wrinkled *domina*—all these poor and pious lambs lead this life of constant martyrdom only for a whim of the great Pachomius."

How various have been the means adopted by human beings to wean themselves from this world in the hope of gaining everlasting felicity! Not content to live in seclusion far away from their fellow-creatures; not content with emaciating their bodies by privations, or lacerating them by self-inflicted tortures, some anchorites, both men and women, so debased themselves as to live in little holes in the earth, and, like the lower animals, to walk on all fours and eat grass and herbs, in imitation of the beasts of the field, and to scamper off to their holes on the approach of a stranger! Some of the grazing anchorites were foolish enough to venture into districts where neither grass nor water was to be had, and they would have died there had they not been rescued by travellers.

When, in the fourth century, Athanasius took some Egyptian monks to Rome—a city afterwards so much identified with monks and monkery—they were looked upon with feelings somewhat akin to contempt and disgust, in consequence of the uncouthness of their dress and uncleanness of their bodies. But these feelings soon gave place to those of respect and reverence. The shirts of goats' hair were now looked upon as a token of sanctity, and the want of cleanliness on the part of the monks as a sign of humility. All classes applauded them. They became respected by noble ladies, who were drawn to them by a strange fascination; reverenced by men who were venerable in years and great in learning; and praised by the populace for the mystery that surrounded them.

Western monachism holds the same relationship to St Benedict as that of the East did to St Anthony. Benedict was born in Umbria, Italy, in 480. When quite a youth he was sent to be educated in Rome, but so dissatisfied was he with the state of society there that at the age of fourteen he went to Sabiaco, to spend a spiritual life in solitude. Here in a cave—afterwards called the Holy Grotto—he passed three years, and his fame having spread abroad, multitudes came to his retreat. He was appointed abbot of a neighbouring monastery, which, however, he soon left, the loose morals of the monks being grievous to a mind so pure as his. After founding twelve cloisters near that place, he founded his famous monastery on Monte Cassino, near Naples, and there in 515 he drew up his *Regula Monachorum*, which ultimately became the common rule of nearly all Western monachism. The order increased rapidly, and the Benedictines have with truth been regarded as the chief agents in the spread of Christianity, civilisation, and learning in this part of the world. It is said that the Benedictines had at one time as many as 37,000 monasteries. The rule of St Benedict was based on the principles of obedience and industry. The periods of meditation and religious service, as well as those of secular employment, were strictly regulated, and when not otherwise employed the monks passed no inconsiderable portion of their time in the scriptorium copying manuscripts for the library, and in consequence of this many of the literary remains of antiquity have been preserved.

Seven centuries later, when the older order of monks had become rich and worldly, St Francis of Assisi, one of the most remarkable men of his age, and who, according to Dean Milman, was the most blameless and gentle of all the saints, instituted a further change in monachism by founding an order of friars which bore his name. The two great characteristics of this order were poverty and humility. He and his followers were to have no property, individually or collectively; and to fulfil literally the precepts of the Great Teacher, they were to go forth to the world without scrip, or purse, and preach the gospel to every creature.

The twelfth century was one of great importance to Scotland. Great social, political, and religious reforms were carried out, and one of the most important factors in this work was the founding of Benedictine and other monasteries. These supplanted the establishments of the old Culdee clergy—the pioneers of Christianity in the country—many of whom had now lapsed from their rule, and had not only married, but had appropriated the possessions of the Church to their own families. The Reformed Church could reckon among its members not only men of learning, but also architects, sculptors, painters, and other skilled artificers. In architectural beauty and gorgeousness of furnishing, their churches far excelled the castles of the barons or the palaces of the king. Even now, on looking on their ruins, hoary with age, one cannot but wonder at the genius that conceived them and the skill of the cunning hands that fashioned them. The common people of those early times, who dwelt in humble houses built of wood, or in mud hovels, must have been spellbound on entering those splendid churches; and the haughty but unlettered barons could not but compare the refinement of the ecclesiastics with the rude manners of their own courts

The chief monasteries were abbeys and priories. They were places of considerable extent and surrounded by high walls. Besides the church, with its vestry and sacristy, there were the conventual buildings, including the chapter-house, the refectory with kitchen, brewhouse, bakehouse, and various stores; a hospitium or guest hall, the library, scriptorium, and treasury. These were generally on the ground floor, and above were the dormitories and the infirmary. In the centre was the cloister court with its alleys, and a passage—or slype, as it was called—led to the cemetery close by. There were officers over the various departments. In abbeys the abbot was, of course, the head, with the prior and sub-prior; the almoner, who distributed the alms, which, by ancient canon law, amounted to a tenth of the whole income of the establishment; the sacristan, who looked after the vestments; the cellarer, who, besides attending to the stores, sometimes acted as cashier; the master of the novices, &c. Their religious services were performed seven times a day, commencing at an early hour, and the remainder of their time was devoted to useful work. The churchmen held the highest offices in the state, and as a rule were more loyal than the nobles. Not only did they give their services in civil affairs, but when duty called they hesitated not to follow their sovereign to the field. We know how the abbot of Inchaffray encouraged the Scottish army at Bannockburn, and how the archbishop of St Andrews and others of the higher clergy fell with their king at Flodden.

The monasteries were generally richly endowed, not only with the teinds or tithes of parishes, called the spirituality, but also with large territories, called the temporality. The land owned by the clergy was the best cultivated in the kingdom. On every barony was a grange, generally managed by a lay brother, and the work was done by the church vassals, who were of several grades. These were the serfs, who could be transferred with the soil on which they wrought; the cottars, each of whom had a piece of land along with his cottage; the husbandmen, who lived on their own farm steadings; also those who held their land by charter and seisin; and above them again were the great vassals, who held a position only inferior to that of the freeholders of the Crown. Wheat, oats, and barley were grown on the lower grounds, and the pasture land afforded an abundant supply of hay. The rearing of sheep also engaged the attention of the churchmen, and the wool from their large and numerous flocks added considerably to the revenues of their establishments. They had their mills, orchards, salmon-fishings, salt-pans, and town houses; in short, everything that could give wealth and influence. Such was the development of monachism. From a small beginning it became a great power. The monasteries in their best days were the centres of religious light and learning, the great civilising agents, the promoters of arts and sciences, and to their last they were the repositories of works of inestimable value. Their chartularies throw much light on the early history of our country, but, unfortunately, many of them have been lost.

Jedburgh Abbey, like all the others, was of considerable extent. It held all the ground south of the royal burgh, between the head of Abbey Close and the foot of Canongate to the river. The conventual buildings occupied the space between the Abbey Church and the river. What is still known as the Abbey Mill was the mill of the convent, and it possessed other mills besides. Between Lady's Yards and the abbey buildings was the original burying ground of the monastery—afterwards called the leigh kirkyard—through which the public road now runs. The principal entrance to the abbey was by the Abbey Close, and this was defended by Dabie's Tower. The entrance by the present churchyard was defended by a tower near to the south corner of the market place, and a third tower defended the entrance by Dean's Close. The extent of this ground was not greatly less than that occupied by the burgh. Besides, almost close by, the canons had their important barony of Ulston, to say nothing of the numerous other properties elsewhere. It will now be our purpose to give, as far as possible, an account of this institution from its rise to its dissolution, and of subsequent events relating thereto.

THE FIRST CHURCH AT JEDBURGH.

"Where in ages dim the sacred hymn
Was chaunted holilie."

A LITTLE before the middle of the ninth century, while the Border districts still formed part of the ancient kingdom of Cumbria, the two Gedworths, and all that belonged to them, were, we are told by Simeon of Durham, gifted to the see of Lindisfarne by Ecgred, who was bishop of that diocese from 830 till 845. One of the Gedworths is now represented by Jedburgh, a royal burgh pleasantly situated on the left bank of the Jed, two miles above its junction with the Teviot. The other is represented only by a modern farm steading and a few grassy mounds of an ancient burying ground some four miles further up the valley, where no sound is now heard save the voice of the peasant, the rippling of the river, or the cooing of the cushat.

In the *Origines Parochiales* eighty-two ways of spelling the name are given, and even that list does not exhaust all the known forms. Chalmers and others have thought that Gedworth means the hamlet or village on the Jed; while Fordun, who calls the town Jedwood, was of opinion that it got its name from the wood or forest on the Jed. The editor of the work referred to says that perhaps the oldest form of the name—Geddewerde—may suggest another derivation. The Rev. Thomas Somerville, D.D., who wrote the Jedburgh portion of the old *Statistical Account of Scotland*, says that the name is said to be derived from the Gadeni, a British tribe which anciently inhabited the whole tract of country that lies between Northumberland and the river Teviot. It was, perhaps, he adds, the capital city belonging to the tribe, and hence obtained the name of Gadburgh or Jedburgh. The modern spelling does not appear, so far as we are aware, till the fifteenth century, although Dr Somerville says that "in a charter granted by William the Lion of Scotland to the abbot and monks of Jedburgh in the year 1165, the name Jedworth and Jedburgh are promiscuously used." A copy of the charter alluded to is given towards the end of this book, and a reference to it will show how far the rev. doctor is correct. Similar statements are made in Scott's *Border Antiquities* in almost the same words.

There can be little doubt that a church existed here in Ecgred's time. Chalmers in his *Caledonia*, Vol. II., p. 132, says that Ecgred built a church for his village of Old Gedworth, and on page 163 he states that "amid the darkness which preceded the dawn of record a manor was laid out lower down the Jed by one of the Earls of Northumberland, and there he built a castle, a church, and a mill, which all distinctly appear in the charters of David I." According to Dempster's *Ecclesiastical History*—a work, however, upon which too much reliance should not be placed—a monastic institution flourished at Jedburgh at the end of the tenth century, and one of the superiors, named Kennoch, was afterwards regarded as a saint. Dempster says that this holy man, by virtue of his unceasing prayers and entreaties, prevailed upon the kings of Scotland and England, when their minds were strongly inclined for war, to maintain peace for a period of ten years! We cannot know to a certainty what kind of structure the earliest church at Jedburgh was, but in all probability it was built of wood and covered with reeds, that being the usual character of churches in this country at that period. The only incident we know in connection with it is recorded by Simeon of Durham, who informs us that about the end of the eleventh century, Eadulf, one of the assassins of Bishop Walcher, was buried in the church of Geddewerde, and that his body was afterwards cast out from thence as execrable by Turgot, the prior and archdeacon of Durham.

About the middle of the tenth century, Cumbria, which up to this time had been ruled by its own kings, lost its independence when it became a tributary principality held of the King of the English by the heir of the King of the Scots.[1] On the accession of Alexander I. to the Scottish throne in 1107, his brother David became Prince of Cumbria, and he was the last who held the title. The Scotland over which Alexander ruled was north of the firths of Forth and Clyde; and David's possessions in Cumbria, says Skene, consisted of the counties of Lanark, Ayr, Renfrew, Dumfries, and Peebles, and his rule extended also over Lothian and Teviotdale, in the counties of Berwick, Roxburgh, and Selkirk. While yet a youth, David accompanied his sister Matilda to the English court on her marriage with Henry I., which took place in 1100, and there he was trained in all the feudal usages and other accomplishments of the English nobility. He married the rich widow of the Earl of Northampton, and by this union he acquired that earldom, together with the honour of Huntington. In 995 the episcopal seat had been removed from Lindisfarne to Durham, and in 1100 this diocese was stripped of Carlisle and Teviotdale. The first public act of Prince David was to restore the fallen bishopric of Glasgow, which was committed to the care of his old preceptor John, called also Achaius, a prelate of great worth and learning. It was through David's instrumentality that the southern part of Teviotdale was annexed to the see of Glasgow. He was, as we have said, an accomplished prince, his residence at the court of England having, according to William of Malmesbury, an English annalist,

---

[1] The *Saxon Chronicle* says that in 945 King Eadmond harried over all Cumberland, and gave it up to Malcolm, King of Scots, on condition that he should be his co-operator both on sea and land. It has been usually assumed, says Skene in his *Celtic Scotland*, that this refers to the district in England called Cumberland alone, but the people termed by the same *Chronicle* the Strathclyde Welsh had now come to be known under the Latin appellation of "Cumbri," and their territory as the land of the Cumbrians, of which Cumberland is simply the Saxon equivalent. There can be little question, he adds, that the tenure by which the Cumbrian kingdom was held by Malcolm was one of fealty towards the King of England, and this seems to be the first occasion on which this relation was established with any reality between them, so far at least as this grant was concerned.

freed him from the rust of Scottish barbarity. In 1124, on the death of his brother Alexander, he succeeded to the Scottish throne as David I., and proved himself in every way worthy of his high position. The Church had never a better friend nor a more liberal benefactor.

THE MONASTERY AS FOUNDED BY DAVID.

PREVIOUS to his accession to the throne David had done much to carry on the reform of the Church which had been commenced by his father, Malcolm Canmore, and his saintly mother, Queen Margaret. About 1118, by the advice of his old friend, John Achaius, he established at Jedburgh a body of Canons Regular, who followed the rule of St Augustine, and who were brought from the abbey of St Quentin, at Beauvais, in France. These canons, who differed from monks only in name, wore a long black cassock, with a white linen rochet over it, and a black open cope, with a square black cap open, instead of a cowl, and they allowed their beards to grow. Lynwood says that some canons wore boots, like monks, and some shoes, like seculars. The Canons Regular were sometimes called Black Canons, from the colour of their dress.

The establishment, it seems, was at first a priory, though Wynton takes no notice of this, but calls it an abbey:—

"A thousand and a hundyre zhere,
And awchtene to rekyne clere,
Gedward and Kelsowe Abbayis twa,
Or Davy was king he founded tha."

Fordun states that the monastery was founded in 1147. The truth appears to be that at the first-mentioned date a priory was built, and that at about the latter date it was raised to the dignity of an abbey. Sir James Dalrymple, who says that he had seen "a copy of the charter of foundation by David," adds, " All that I can say of this abbacy is that it is probable it was anciently a religious house or monastery, and some time in the possession of the Church of Durham, and so more of the nature of a Dunelmian than Culdean monastery. It was governed at first by a prior. I think the priory has been changed to an abbacy about the end of the reign of King David." David died in 1153. In 1139, one Daniel was styled "Prior de Geddwrda;" and Osbert, who was also called prior in 1150, is alluded to in charters of Malcolm IV. as abbot of Gedworth. The death of Osbert, which took place in 1174, is noticed in the *Melrose Chronicle*, where he is styled "primus abbas de Geddeworthe."

We think that the extent of the church of the priory may with some certainty be ascertained by an examination of the present ruins. Taking the Early Norman work for our guide, we would say that it consisted of a choir of two bays in length and three storeys in height, having an apsidal termination towards the east; a chapel on each side of the choir, and two transepts, with a tower over the intersection. At this early period the choir or chancel was generally only about one square in length, and Norman towers seldom rose more than a square above the other wall-heads. There is no indication of a nave having been built at this period. It was quite a customary thing for only a portion of the more important churches to be erected and fitted up for worship before the other parts were commenced; and in a few instances in this country—such as the Collegiate Church at Roslin, and the Church of the Holy Trinity, Edinburgh—the buildings were never completed. The apse and Norman clerestory would be removed when the chancel was about to be enlarged, shortly after the erection of the nave, to which reference is made a little further on. A small portion of the original clerestory wall, with pieces of two string-courses, and a fragment of corbelling, may still be seen in a portion of the old wall at the north-east corner of the tower.

In the early work the lower arches, which are square-edged, are very peculiar, springing as they do not from capitals but from corbels in the sides of the round pillars; and hence it has been suggested that those arches were an after-thought, and inserted after the completion of the zig-zag moulded arches above. In regard, at least, to some of the arches there are indications that would support this idea, notably in that to the right at the entrance

JEDBURGH ABBEY, NORMAN ARCHES IN CHOIR

to the north transept, where it is quite evident that the pillars have been cut for the insertion of the corbels and arch mouldings. A similar plan was followed by Abbot Thomas Cranston more than three centuries afterwards, when the east arch of the south aisle of the nave was built. When he rebuilt the great south-west pier, provision was made for the support of one end of the arch, but the Norman pillar opposite had to be cut into so that a corbel might be inserted to support the other end. An arrangement somewhat similar is found in Christ Church Cathedral, Oxford, and also at Romsey, in Hampshire. The arches, when seen from the interior of the choir, appear as if of a single order, but towards the aisles they are triply recessed. Those in the triforium are subdivided. The original subdividing arches, with rounded voussoirs, are seen in one of the bays on the south side, and are semicircular in form, while those on the north side have been replaced by pointed ones, and the putting in of additional shafts has further changed the character and marred the simplicity of the early style. These alterations seem to have been made so as to give support to the great north-east pier of the tower.

The original work can be easily distinguished by its heavy round pillars and semicircular arches. Some of the arches are plain and square-edged, while in others the square edge has given place to the bowtell moulding or to the zig-zag ornament. The bases of the pillars are plain, with a small chamfer at the upper edge, and the capitals are either cushion-shaped or simply notched down towards the neck-mould. A capital, with stiff, rudely-formed volutes—apparently an attempt to imitate the Ionic—may be seen supporting a small arch in the south transept, where the stair ascends to the tower. The abacus is always square, with a hollow chamfer at the upper edge, and some of the hood-moulds and string-courses partake much of the same character. The other mouldings are mostly round, like the bowtell—or, as it is sometimes called, the Norman edge roll—along with shallow hollows. None of the windows of this early period remain, though the jamb of one of them is seen built up in the east wall of the south chapel, and the jambs of two others are seen on the remaining fragment of the east wall of the north chapel. The spring of the arch of the lowest of these still exists. Norman windows were but a subordinate feature in the buildings. It may be mentioned that the strength of the massive round piers is more apparent than real, as some of them at least—those of the tower—consist of an outer course of ashlar and a core of loose material that had never been properly grouted. Some towers of the Norman period in England have given way in consequence of their having been built in this manner, and in Jedburgh it has been found necessary to shore up the Norman piers of the tower to prevent a collapse. The roofs of the choir chapels were of stone, and were intersected by groin ribs, but the larger spaces were covered with wood. The church was dedicated to the Virgin Mary.

ERECTION OF THE NAVE AND EXTENSION OF THE CHOIR.

From the foundation of the first church to the completion of the work above described a period of three hundred years had elapsed, and though the history of that period is very obscure, it is certain that during that time important changes had taken place in this district. An independent kingdom, long ruled by its own kings, had disappeared, and its territory, which was of considerable extent, had been taken by two powerful neighbours. The boundaries between Scotland and England, something like what they are at present, had been defined, and strong castles had been erected to defend them. One of these was at Jedburgh. A more learned priesthood had taken the place of the earlier teachers of Christianity. The Church itself was receiving more marks of royal favour, and a brighter era seemed approaching. The newly-established body of canons at Jedburgh had their house richly endowed by the saintly David, who frequently resided in the castle, both before and after his accession to the throne. These gifts were confirmed by his son, Prince Henry, and were added to by Malcolm IV., William the Lion, Robert I., and other liberal donors.

It is reasonable to suppose that soon after this religious establishment was raised to the higher position of an abbey, the church would receive important additions, as became its dignity. It is extremely probable, therefore, that the whole of the nave and the pointed part of the choir would be built between 1150 and 1230, so that at the time of the marriage of Alexander III., which took place here in 1285, the church of Jedburgh Abbey would be one of the finest buildings in the country. The style of the architecture of these portions agrees with the period mentioned, affording exquisite examples of the transition between Norman and Early English. In the nave the transition is shown in a very marked degree. There are on each side three tiers of pillars and arches, possessing a grace and lightness, and a beauty of general outline, much and deservedly admired. The basement storey consists of clustered pillars which support deeply-moulded pointed arches; in the triforium are semi-circular arches subdivided by pointed ones; while the clerestory is a detached arcade of thirty-six arches, also pointed, the wall behind every alternate two being pierced for windows. In the lower storeys the abacus, with only one exception, is square, as in all the older work, but in the clerestory the square edges are cut off, indicating the desire that had set in for new forms. The exception referred to is in the triforium, near the centre, on the north side. It consists of a series of rounds, like many in Early English work, while the capital in this particular instance is not unlike the capitals in the south doorway, to which we shall afterwards refer. In the nave the other capitals, which are all more or less foliated, exhibit great diversity of outline. This diversity may be accounted for by the fact that in those early times the master mason, or architect, planned the general design, and left the workmen, who were all highly skilled, to work out the details. "The masons, who worked from the architect's design," says a recent writer on the subject, "were not the mere human machines that modern workmen too generally are, but men who, in carrying out an idea imparted to them, could stamp an individuality of their own on every stone." A curious circumstance is, that while in the east part of the nave the subdividing arches are supported on four shafts, they are in the western part supported on two. The change takes place just about the middle. The tympanum is, in almost every instance, pierced with a circular opening (square, however, on the outside); the only exceptions—two quatrefoils and two elliptical or oval-shaped openings—being on the south side. These four are further distinguished by being ornamented with small balls all round the openings. We may here incidentally mention, as showing the great diversity of workmanship visible throughout the building, that on each side of the nave the westermost arch on

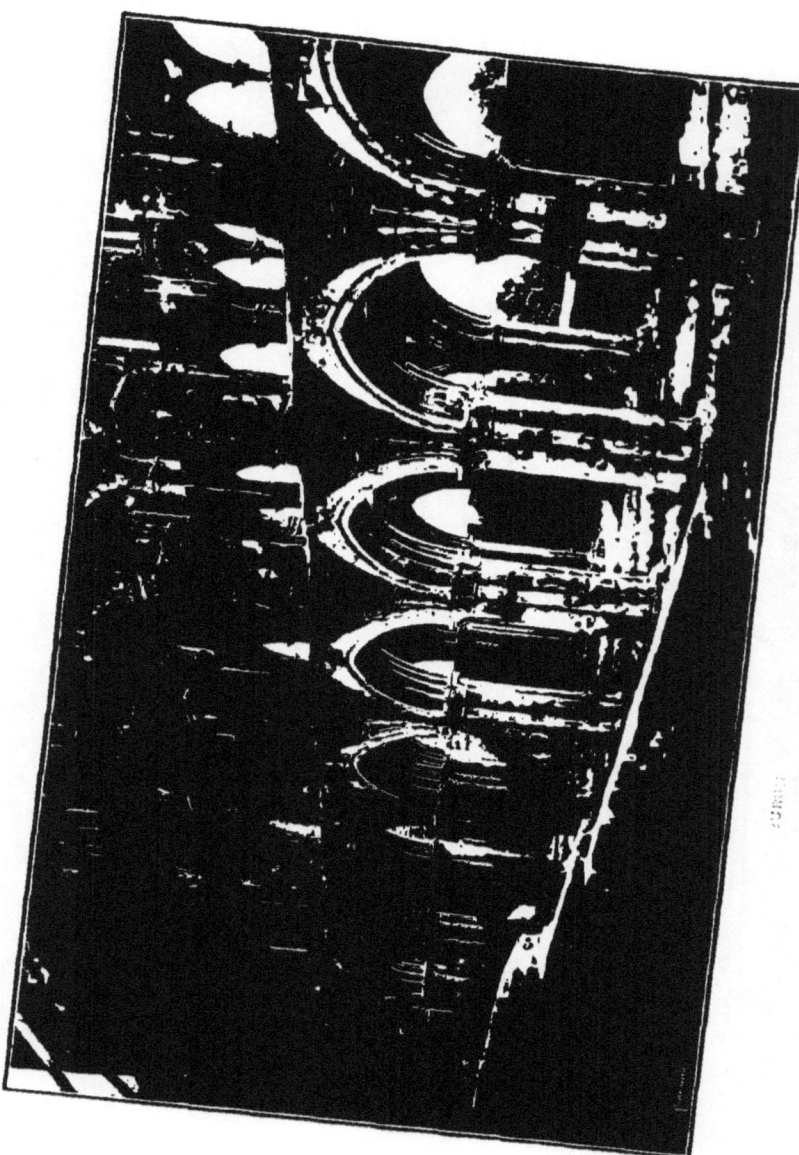

the basement storey has two more mouldings than any of the others. The semicircular arch second from the tower on the north side seems never to have been subdivided, the soffit mouldings being carried round unbroken. Why there should have been this departure from the general plan it is not easy to determine, but as the place is opposite to the doorway through which the canons entered the church, may not this have been the position of the organ? It is worthy of remark that, in the nave, not only are most of the arches pointed, but the mouldings in the lower storeys, as also the clustered pillars on the ground floor, are of the same character. It will also be observed that the bases of the pillars here have, like the capitals, assumed a more advanced form than those in the choir. The mouldings in the clerestory, however, are round, like those in the choir. The original north aisle wall, of which only a fragment remains attached to the north transept, was pierced with a number of one-light windows. The jamb of one of them still remains, and they seem to have been similar to those at the sides of the west doorway. The south aisle was lighted with a kind of dormer windows which rose from near the top of the wall, and pierced the lay-to roof of the triforium. The sills of three of them are still seen. As dormers are understood not to have been known until about the fourteenth century, this would suggest that the present was not the original south aisle wall, but one built probably at the time of the restoration of the conventual buildings some time after the year 1300. There is evidently a break in the masonry near the old cloister doorway. A considerable portion of this wall, as well as that on the north side, has recently been restored. It is quite evident, from various considerations, that neither the nave nor the choir was ever covered with a stone-vaulted roof, as was the case in most of the later buildings. The groined vaults required to be poised with great skill, due regard being observed in the counteracting of their outward thrust, and hence it was that the builders contented themselves with the vaulting of side aisles, and the like, until they gained more confidence, when they threw the vaults over places of much greater extent. The south transept had been covered with the cylindrical or barrel vaulting of stone, while groined vaulting was thrown over the side aisles of the nave, as well as over the side chapels of the choir. The cloister doorway (at the east end of the south aisle wall), which is of transition Norman character, possesses features of interest of no ordinary kind. Billings, in his *Baronial and Ecclesiastical Antiquities of Scotland*, while referring to this, remarks that few doorways, even of the fifteenth century, are more delicately, although they may be more profusely, decorated; and Sir Gilbert G. Scott says that this and the great western doorway "are two of the most exquisite gems of architectural art in this island." The cloister doorway is less deeply recessed and less elaborate in detail than that in the western gable, but it possesses a chasteness of design and a delicacy of execution altogether unique. This doorway having become very much decayed, the present Marquess of Lothian, the noble proprietor of the abbey, ordered a *facsimile* of this beautiful piece of architectural art to be made, so that a faithful copy might be preserved, and the work was, under the direction of Dr Robert Rowand Anderson, architect, Edinburgh, completed in a manner that cannot fail to satisfy the most severe critic. The new doorway has been put up on the same side of the nave, to the west of the old one. The mouldings generally are extremely bold and beautiful, and the foliated capitals, which are deeply undercut and show the foliage in high relief, are protected by a circular abacus. In the arch the first order inside the label mould is entirely composed of the chevron ornament, while the second is covered with representations of human figures, grotesque animals, birds, and foliage, alternately arranged. There are representations of David slaying the bear, and of Samson tearing asunder the jaws of the lion. On the left side are two nondescript animals with human heads and bodies like birds, the tails terminating with foliage, as is common in work of the same period. There are other nondescript animals of different forms. The third order consists of a pointed bowtell, and the fourth is a kind of zig-zag moulding, highly decorated with carved foliage. The western doorway, as has already been stated, is more deeply recessed and more elaborate in

JEDBURGH

BURGH ABBEY, WEST DOORWAY

detail than the other, but it has also been much defaced. Like that already noticed, this doorway is semicircular in form, and the chief mouldings are the chain, the fish-bone, and the chevron, with an abundance of foliage, representations of human heads, and of grotesque birds. In one of the hollow mouldings in the arch the undeveloped dog-tooth and the star are alternately arranged; while down the jambs the nail-head is seen in conjunction with the chevron. Here are the square abacus and foliated capitals, but the shafts which formerly supported these are now gone. Over the doorway are three empty niches, with trefoil arches. Arches of this character are not of frequent occurrence in work of so early a period. Above these is a large one-light window, 18 feet 10 inches in height, and 5 feet 8 inches in breadth, with semicircular arch, there being an attached arcade of a few pointed arches on each side. Near the top of the gable is a beautiful St Catherine's wheel of a later period. At each side of the doorway is a one-light window, with semicircular arch. These windows have originally had jamb shafts, but they, like six others in the attached arcade alluded to, have disappeared. At the north-west corner of the gable are two Norman buttresses, which, like all those in very early work, project little from the face of the wall, and hence they have sometimes been not inaccurately called "strip pilasters."

Some have thought that the lower part of this gable, with its Norman doorway, its Norman windows, and its Norman buttresses, must be older than the nave, and that therefore an earlier nave must have existed. Such, however, is an erroneous supposition. In the first place, in not a few instances the Norman doorway is found even in Early English buildings, as if the architects of that time were loath to leave what they could not expect to improve; and, in the second place, the nave of Jedburgh Abbey, as we have already shown, is wholly of transition Norman character. It is no less curious than instructive to observe how gradually the one style runs into the other. Rickman, who did more, perhaps, than any other man for the classification of the various styles of Gothic architecture, says: "Many pure Norman works have pointed arches.

The square abacus, however, may be taken as the best mark. The pointed arch, in its incipient state, exhibited a change of form only, whilst the accessories and details remained the same as before; and although this change gradually led to the early pointed style in its pure state, with mouldings and features altogether distinct from those of the Norman, and to the general disuse, in the thirteenth century, of the semicircular arch, it was for a while so intermixed as, from its first appearance to the close of the twelfth century, to constitute that state of transition called the semi-Norman." Had there been an earlier nave in Jedburgh Abbey some portion of it would doubtless have remained. The early builders were not strictly careful as to uniformity, and hence we find that, when a chapel or aisle was partially destroyed, it was rebuilt, not in its original style, but in that prevalent at the time of the restoration; and the new parts are easily discernible by their different character. It is also worthy of remark that the fragment of the original side aisle wall of the nave adjoining the north transept has a base similar to that of the west gable. The whole of the base and the lower part of the wall were restored in 1876. Another consideration which bears on the probability of there having been no earlier nave is that, from the time of David I.—indeed, we may say from that of Malcolm III.—to the death of Alexander III., there had been a period of great prosperity, such as Scotland had never before witnessed; the arts of peace and industry flourished in a manner never before experienced. In short, it was a time of building up rather than of throwing down.

The composition of the pointed part of the choir differs considerably from that of the nave, and seems in some respects a nearer approach to Early English. The clerestory, only part of which now remains, had consisted of a detached arcade, each alternate arch being larger than the others for the insertion of the windows. Under this, to the east of the side chapels, was another arcade of a similar kind, but the arches and lights were much larger; and under this again was an attached arcade. In the upper storey on each side are what are called stilted arches, the spring of the arch being considerably above the capital. This part of the building is, unfortunately, much dilapidated, but sufficient remains to show its beautiful arrangement, and to give some idea to the initiated of its grand effect when entire. Something like the same arrangement would, we doubt not, be continued round the east end. On the north side some of the higher capitals are severely plain, while most of those on the south side are foliated. The windows in this part, which are all single pointed lights, have on the outside the round bowtell moulding rising to the top of the arches without a break, and over this is a label moulding. The windows, mouldings, and the upright chamfered buttresses which support the walls, partake largely of the Early English character; but some of the other details, such as the capitals and abacus, represent older forms.

EVENTS BETWEEN 1220 AND 1285.

BESIDES attending to the internal affairs of their convent, the abbots had to attend to many other matters. In 1208 there was a final agreement made in the King's Court at Carlisle on the morrow of St Andrew, before Adam de Port and other Justices, between Duncan de Lasceles and Christina, his wife, complainants, and Hugh, abbot of Geddeworthe, deforciant, regarding the advowson of the church of Bastenethwait. The recognizance of the last presentation was produced between them in court, viz., that the said complainants admitted the advowson of the church to be the right of the abbot and his church of Geddeworthe, by the gift of Waldef, son of Gospatric, father of Christina, to be held by the abbot and his successors and the church of Geddeworthe in pure and perpetual alms; and the said abbot granted to Duncan and Christina, and their heirs, participation for ever in all the benefits and prayers of the church of Geddeworthe (*Calendar of Documents Relating to Scotland*, Vol. I.).

A dispute having occurred between the bishop of Glasgow and the canons of Jedburgh regarding certain churches and other matters, the questions in dispute were referred to five arbiters, who met in the church of Nisbet in 1220, and, after full deliberation, decided in favour of the bishop. The decision was to the effect that the abbot and canons were to obey the bishop, or his official, in all canonical matters; that the chaplain of the church of Jedburgh was to yield fit obedience to them when they should come to perform episcopal offices in that church; that the abbot was, according to ancient custom, to attend in person at the festival of the dedication of the church of Glasgow, or, if prevented by reasonable excuse, to send a suitable procurator; and that he should attend synod when summoned. It was resolved in regard to the church of Longnewton that the vicarage should be a benefice of eight merks, or the altarages, with the lands and all other pertinents, in the option of the vicar when the charge should be vacant, he paying yearly half a stone of wax in recognition at the Feast of St James; that the residue should go to the use of the canons, and that until the charge should be vacant the canons should be responsible to the extent of one-half for the episcopal dues, and for the sustentation of the priest, whom they should present to the bishop or his official. It was ordained that in this, as in other parishes, the canons were to have one acre of land for storing their corn, in a proper place, saving only the messuage of the vicar. It was determined that the vicar of Hobkirk should have, in name of vicarage, ten merks, or the whole altarage, with its lands and pertinents, and that as an acknowledgment he should pay to the canons half a stone of wax at the Feast of St James, and that the whole of the residue should go to the canons, saving the right of Master Ada Ovidius. In regard to the church of Rule Abbatis (Abbotrule), it was agreed that its fruits should belong to the vicar, who should pay to the canons yearly in recognition the sum of 5s. at the Feast of St James. The corn tithes of the church of Hownam were to be given up for the use of the canons, but the vicar was to get £10, or the whole of the altarage, at his option, on his giving annually at the Feast of St James a stone of wax to the monastery, reserving the right of Master Hugh de Potton, archdeacon of Glasgow. It was agreed that the taxation of the churches of Oxnam, Eckford, and that of St Martin of Lidel should remain as it had been fixed by the bishop's charter (*Chartulary of Glasgow.* See Chalmers' *Caledonia*, Vol II.). In 1237 certain rights of the canons in Hownam were disputed by the monks of Melrose, but the dispute was brought to a close on the canons allowing the monks' lands of Hunedune and Raschawe, in the parish of Hownam, to be tithe-free, and agreeing to find a chaplain to pray for the souls of William, the son of John of Hownam, and Donancia, his wife, and all the faithful departed, in whatever place the bishop of Glasgow should appoint.

On 2nd September 1255 King Alexander III. wrote to his

father-in-law, Henry III. of England, then at Sprouston, that at the instance of the council of his own magnates, including the abbots of Jedburgh and Kelso, &c., he had removed the bishops of Glasgow and Dunblane and others from his council and their offices in consequence of their demerits; and that by the same advice he had ordered others to his council, and to be regents of his kingdom, and guardians of himself and his queen (*Cal. of Doc. Rel. to Scot.*). Alexander had succeeded to the throne in 1249, when he was only eight years of age, and the tender age of the Scottish sovereign enabled Henry to prosecute successfully for some time his schemes for obtaining control over the Scottish kingdom. The spirited conduct of the youthful monarch, however, was not long in convincing his wily relative that his ambitious designs would prove of little avail. On 9th December of that year Henry granted to the abbot of Jedburgh that till after the expiry of three years from the Feast of Christmas he and his "familiar men" should not be distrained within the king's dominions for the transgressions of another in which they were not culpable, nor for any debt for which they were neither sureties nor principals (*ibid.*).

In the following year, King Alexander, by his envoys, the abbot of Jedburgh and William de Hay, convened a parliament at Stirling, and asked Henry to send some of his "provident and discreet men" thereto. Henry, for reasons given, declined to send any to that parliament, and asked that another should be held at a more convenient time and place (*ibid.*).

A regency having been appointed which included only those of the English party, some unpleasantness arose from an attempt to rule Scotland by the nominees of the English king. The Comyns and their accomplices did their best to oppose them, and Bishop Gameline,[1] who had been removed from his see, induced the Pope to

---

[1] Gameline was elected bishop of St Andrews in 1255, and consecrated on St Stephen's Day by the Pope. He was a man of good repute, but became disagreeable to the court because he would not relax a soldier of the king whom he had excommunicated without previous satisfaction. It is also related how this bishop was banished from the king's councillors because he would

excommunicate the councillors of the youthful king. The ceremony was performed by Clement, bishop of Dunblane, and the abbots of Jedburgh and Melrose, in the abbey of Cambuskenneth, and repeated in every church and chapel in the kingdom, by bell, book, and candle (*Melrose Chronicle*). None but the most resolute could at that time brave the anathema of the Church of Rome, and few there were who would boldly exclaim—

> "Bell, book, and candle shall not drive me back,
> When gold and silver becks me to come on."

It was a bold step this of the abbot of Jedburgh, with his brother of Melrose, to assist the bishop in excommunicating and accursing those councillors; to give up their bodies and souls to the devil; to curse them in all their relationships, whether civil or sacred; to ask God to put their names out of the Book of Life, as they (the priests) put out the candle, and to pray that as the candle was put out of the sight of men, so might the souls of those who were anathematized be cast from the sight of God into the deepest pit of hell. As a fit conclusion to all this the bell was rung as for the dead.

On 22nd May 1265 King Henry wrote to all bailiffs, &c., to say that as the abbot of Jedburgh and other envoys of the King of Scotland were on their way, he willed that they come to him at Hereford, where he then was, and granted them safe conduct from that Day of Pentecost till the quinzaine of the Holy Trinity next (*Cal. of Doc. Rel. to Scot.*, Vol. I.).

Between 1264-66, Hugh de Abernethy, viscount or sheriff of Roxburgh, gave in an account, from which was deducted xix lb. vijs. vjd., remitted as surety of a certain man of the abbot of Jedworth for war done on the Border (*Exchequer Rolls of Scotland*, Vol. I., p. 29).

At the Cumberland assize, on 12th November 1266, inquiries

---

not give consent to their bad advice, and because he would not advance a sum of money for the purchase of the bishopric. . . . He went to Rome and pleaded his cause before the Pope, and the Pope gave sentence in his behalf (Keith's *Catalogue of Scottish Bishops*).

were made as to who presented the last parson deceased to the church of Arturet, vacant, which Johanna de Estoteville claimed against the abbot of Jedburgh. The abbot, by his attorney, said that the church was not vacant, but full, and that he and his convent had held it *proprios usus* for twenty years past and more as their own patronage (*Cal. of Doc. Rel. to Scot.*, Vol. I.).

The abbey possessed considerable lands in Northumberland, and it appears from the *Iter of Wark* that the abbot had certain law pleas with William of Bellingham. At a court held at Wark, in Tyndale, in the thirty-first year of the reign of Alexander, King of Scotland (1280), before Thomas Randolf, Symon Fraser, Hugh de Persby, and David Thorwald, justiciars, there appeared for the settlement of mutual grievances the abbot of Jedburgh and William de Bellingham, the former complaining of the conduct of William de Bellingham—who appears to have been the royal forester in Tyndale, holding two parts of the manor of Bellingham by service of the King of the Scots throughout his whole forest of Tyndale—in the right of common pasturage, besides a certain place of his called Hesleyside, and claiming £14 of damage; and the latter claiming that the abbot should be made to return to him a certain cirograph charter which he had delivered up to him for inspection at the abbot's court at the Leye, and which he had never returned, and claiming £20 of damages. The result was that William undertook, for himself and his heirs, to repair and maintain his ditches and hedges (*fossis et hayes*)[1] of Hesleyside, and granted to the abbot and his successors, and their tenants of Evelingham, the right of common pasturage of Hesleyside. He also remitted and upgave all right

---

[1] Cosmo Innes, in his *Scotland in the Middle Ages*, states that after the death of Alexander III., which took place in 1286, John Cummin rendered his account as bailiff of the king's manor of Jedworth, which included "Item, for 900 perches of ditch and hedge (*fosse et haye*) constructed about both the wood and meadows of Jedworth, 116/6ᵈ." Innes says, "I think I cannot be mistaken in translating these words *ditch and hedge;* and if so, you have by far the earliest instance of such a fence on record." The reader will observe that the instance given above is several years earlier.

and claim to the annual payment of thirteen bolls of meal and 4s. silver, and the pasturage of two mares with their following of two years, the cirographs between Nicholas, quondam abbot of Jedeworthe, predecessor of the then abbot, remaining, nevertheless, in full force. The abbot, on his side, upgave to William and his heirs the right of common pasturage which he had for forty mares with their following of two years in Bellingham, Wardlaw, and Greenacres, without prejudice to the abbot's right of common pasture in the said towns for forty cows and their following of one year, according to the tenor of the charter of Alan, son of Wolfinus, grandfather of the aforesaid William, drawn up in the church of St Mary of Jedeworth.

A ROYAL MARRIAGE IN THE ABBEY.

WHEN Alexander III. was married to Jolande, daughter of the Count de Dreux, Jedburgh was chosen, on account of the beauty of the district, as the place most fitting for the celebration of the nuptials. There was rejoicing throughout all Scotland on that occasion, as the king was deservedly one of the most beloved monarchs who had ever sat upon the throne. One day in October 1285, as the noonday sun shone brightly on the forest trees, which had assumed some of the fainter tints of autumn, there might have been seen approaching Jedburgh from the north a long train of horsemen, numbering several hundreds, with banners fluttering in the gentle breeze. Most of these horsemen are clad in bright armour, partially hid by their loosely-worn riding cloaks, and the horses are richly caparisoned. In that train are the chief nobles of France and Scotland, besides knights and other persons of distinction. A few ladies are among them. The tallest horseman near the front is the king; the fairest of the ladies is the beautiful Jolande. They are hourly expected in the burgh. The soldiers from the battlements of the castle watch their approach, and the canons are on the lookout from the top of the abbey tower. The cavalcade has reached the northern port, and as the king appears within the gate he is greeted with a hearty cheer, and the bells ring forth merry peals. Never before was there such a sight on the Borders as when the nobles rode up the steep street on their prancing steeds to the castle at the top of the town. The streets are thronged, and every piece of vantage ground is crowded with spectators eager to witness this display of pomp and magnificence, and to get a glimpse of the youthful bride. Again and again is heard the ringing cheer; the gates of the castle are thrown open, and soon the gay cavalcade is within the walls. For a while there is no further sign of the presence of royalty, but the town still presents an unusual aspect. People go to and fro with eyes ever and anon turned towards the castle. The abbey bell begins to peal, and now there issues from the castle a more splendid procession than had entered it but two hours ago. A few minutes more and the abbot is doing obeisance to his king at the door of the abbey church, and the grand procession moves slowly up the nave, with its long tiers of clustered pillars and graceful arches. A subdued light enters through the long lancet windows at the further end of the chancel, and falls softly on the high altar. A few figures are moving silently along the detached arcade above, and several are looking from the galleries over the choir chapels. The deep tones of the organ which have been resounding through the aisles die away; the royal bride and bridegroom stand before the altar, and the abbot proceeds with the marriage ceremony. The scene is an imposing one. Yonder, near the king, are the great officers of state, with robes and insignia of amazing splendour. The king himself wears a jewelled girdle and robes of purple velvet, hooded with ermine and embroidered with gold. Many of the nobles are somewhat similarly attired; others are clad in mail. The ladies are dressed in the most costly silks, profusely decorated. The head of the bride is graced with a golden circlet, set with pearls and precious stones. The abbot and other church dignitaries have donned their richest vestments, and the church itself has been gaily decorated for this auspicious occasion. But while we gaze with wonder and admiration on so imposing a spectacle, the interesting ceremony is over, and the august assembly returns to the castle.

A grand evening banquet was held in the great hall of the abbey, but the mirth and hilarity of the company were suddenly brought to a close by the appearance of a spectre, which was looked upon as an evil omen, and after events tended rather to confirm than to remove the prevailing opinion. One version of the story, as given by Fordun, is as follows:—" In the midst of the royal banquet a sort of theatrical masque, which had been previously arranged, entered the hall, and proceeded through the middle of it, between the parties of guests that sat on either side. First came a band of revellers, playing upon various musical instruments, and accompanied with splendid pageants; and after them a party who exhibited their skill and agility in a military dance, with a variety of movements and gesticulations. The procession was closed by an unexpected figure, whose mysterious and singular appearance startled the beholders, who were in doubt whether they saw a human being or a phantom, for, like a shadow, it seemed to glide rather than walk. While the whole company gazed on this ill-omened visitor with increasing disgust, it suddenly vanished, leaving them impressed with a gloomy anxiety, which ill disposed them to renew the interrupted sports and revelry."

Heywood, in his *Hierarchie of the Blessed Angels*, while alluding to the same event, says:—

> "In the mid revels, the first ominous night
> Of their espousals, when the moon shone bright,
> With lighted tapers, the king and queen leading
> The curious measures, lords and ladies treading
> The self-same strains, the king looks back by chance
> And spies a strange intruder fill the dance,
> Namely, a mere anatomy, quite bare,
> His naked limbs both without flesh and hair
> (As we decipher Death), who stalks about,
> Keeping true measure till the dance be out.
> The king with all the rest, affrighted stand,
> The spectre vanished, and then strict command
> Was given to break up revels; each 'gan fear
> The other, and presage disaster near."

Thus ended the rejoicings which had been commenced with so much joy and pageantry, and the sudden death of the king, which occurred shortly afterwards, more than fulfilled the worst fears which had arisen in consequence of the appearance of the ill-omened visitor. Alexander's death proved most disastrous to Scotland. Immediately after came the disputed succession, which was followed closely by the War of Independence, and the national prosperity with which Scotland had been so long blessed was for a considerable time completely checked—

"So swift trod sorrow on the heels of joy."

In the following lines, one of the oldest fragments of Scottish poetry, preserved in Wynton's *Chronicle*, reference is made to the altered condition of Scotland after the death of Alexander:—

> "Quhen Alysander oure kyng was dede
> That Scotland held in luwe and lé,
> Away wes sons of ale and brede,
> Of wyne and wax, of gamyn and glé;
> Oure gold wes changyd into lede,
> Cryst borne into virgynite,
> Succour Scotland and remede,
> That stad is in perplexyte."

Fordun, alluding to Alexander III., says that in his time "the Church flourished, its ministers were treated with reverence, vice was openly discouraged, cunning and treachery were trampled under foot, injury ceased, and the reign of virtue, truth, and justice was maintained throughout the land."

THE EFFECTS OF THE WAR OF INDEPENDENCE ON THE ABBEY.

ALEXANDER having left no family of his own, the rival claims of Bruce and Baliol to the inheritance of the throne were set up, and when the Scottish Parliament had agreed to refer the matter to the arbitration of Edward I. of England, the abbot of Jedburgh was one of three commissioners sent by Parliament to the English king. An early chronicler places this embassy in 1286, but Tytler thinks it might be a little later.

A meeting of the Estates of the realm having been held in 1284 to settle the succession, in the event of the king having no direct heir, a resolution was come to, by Alexander's request, that Margaret of Norway, his granddaughter, should be recognised as heir to the crown. After the king's untimely death, Margaret was accordingly chosen, and Edward lost no time in projecting a marriage between his own son, the Prince of Wales, and the "Maid of Norway." The country was pleased with the proposal, and in 1289 a meeting of the Estates of Scotland was held at Brigham, at which the abbot of Jedburgh was present, when a letter was drawn up and sent to Edward approving of the marriage. A similar letter was sent to Eric, King of Norway. In the following year the abbot attended another meeting of the Estates at the same place, when a treaty was entered into with six plenipotentiaries from England in regard to the matter. However, the sudden death of the young queen—she was only in the eighth year of her age—frustrated the scheme. The disputed succession, which resulted in Baliol being awarded the crown by Edward I., who now openly declared himself to be Lord Paramount of Scotland, is too well known to all readers of Scottish history to require repetition here. For some time afterwards there seems to have been reason to fear that the English king would, as he threatened, bring under his dominion the realm of Scotland in the same way as he had subdued the kingdom of Wales. On the 6th of July 1292—the year in which he placed Baliol on the Scottish throne—King Edward directed William Comyn, Keeper of Selkirk Forest, to send in his name six fat bucks to the abbot of Jedburgh (*Rotuli Scotiæ*); and in December of the same year the abbot was, with other dignitaries, present at Newcastle when Baliol acknowledged Edward to be his feudal superior, and did homage to him as Lord Paramount.

Within the diocese of Durham, in the same year, the following sums, among others, were taxed in order to give the tithes to King Edward :—Abbot of Jedworth, £16 ; abbot of Kelso, in Rolkeopes, £7, 1s. 4d.; and abbots of Melrose and Tholopes, £8, 19s. (Hodgeson's *History of Northumberland*, Part III., Vol. II., p. 354).

At this early period it was not unusual for valuable documents to be deposited in monasteries for their safe keeping, and it is interesting to note that, among other parchments found in Edinburgh Castle in 1292, and ordered by Edward I. to be delivered to King John Baliol, was one entitled "A Letter of William de Fentone, Andrew de Bosco, and David de Graham, acknowledging receipt from Master William Wyscard, archdeacon of St Andrews and chancellor to the king, of certain documents deposited in the abbey of Geddeworth by umquhile John Biset, the son of Sir John Biset " (*Acts of the Scottish Parliament*, Vol. I.).

In the extracts from the account of the keeper of the royal wardrobe there is an entry, of date 2nd November 1295, to the following effect: "ccxix l. vjs. viij$^{d.}$ from the abbot of Geddeworth of the pence of the papal tenth collected in the diocese of Glasgow, and deposited in the aforesaid abbey " (*Hist. Doc. Rel. to Scot.*, Vol. II.).

The principal fortresses in Scotland having in 1291 been placed in Edward's hand by his own request, so that he might be the better able to give effect to his decision in respect to the rival claims, these were restored when John Baliol was placed on the throne in the following year. In 1295, however, Edward demanded, as a pledge of security, that the Scots should live at peace with England while he was at war with France, that the towns and castles of Berwick, Roxburgh, and Jedburgh should be under English control. Baliol, having by this time found out that his sovereignty was merely nominal, and that the wily Edward wished simply to use him as a tool, refused to comply with the demand. He renounced his allegiance, and entered into a treaty with France that same year, and this led to a war between England and Scotland which resulted in the overthrow of Baliol, and the resignation of his kingdom in July 1296 into the hands of Edward, who then attempted to govern in his own absolute right.

On 27th April 1296 a writ was issued ordering that no Scotsman remain on the lands of Scotsmen in England, and among these are mentioned the lands belonging to the abbey of Jedburgh (*ibid.*). In August of the same year the abbots of Jedburgh, Melrose, and Kelso swore fealty to Edward at Berwick, after which they had restored to them their properties, which had been forfeited. These writs were addressed to the sheriffs of seven counties in Scotland, and to the sheriffs of Northumberland and Cumberland. At this time all Scotland may be said to have been under the power of the English king. In the same year Edward requested by letter that Thomas de Byrdelye, clerk, who had been recently mutilated by the Scots in Northumberland, should be admitted into the abbey of Jedburgh for life. Morton suggests, and not without reason, that he had been sent as a spy upon the canons. In June of the following year Edward issued a writ to the sheriff of Northumberland for levying debts connected with Scotland, and for recovering arrears drawn by certain ecclesiastical houses due to the English exchequer, and among others the abbot of Jedburgh was due viijl. for arrears of the moiety granted to the king by the clergy (*ibid.*).

In 1297 Edward instructed Brian Fitz-Allan, Governor of Scotland, that when any ecclesiastical vacancy should occur of no higher value than forty merks yearly he should present it to some member of the Church of England; but Edward reserved the higher offices for his own presentation, and we know that he had already presented William de Jarum to the office of abbot of Jedburgh (see Superiors of the Abbey). All this, of course, was to secure more influence to England. The abbot and convent, along with Sir Ive de Aldeburge, offered, in 1298, to undertake the custody and repair of the castle of Jedburgh, as they understood that the Constable had told the king that he could not keep it without having the forest of Jedburgh. The abbot and Sir Ive petitioned the king to the effect that as he had awarded them by word of mouth at Roxburgh that the forest should continue in their keeping, who were farmers of their lord the king, and as the Constable had disturbed them in the same, they hoped he would provide a remedy (In Public Record Office, and printed in *Hist. Doc. Rel. to Scot.*, Vol. II.).

The cruelty with which Edward enforced his unjust claim was so great that it naturally aroused the indignation of all classes in Scotland, with the exception of the higher nobility, who belonged to the Norman race, and who were too much under the influence of the usurper. It only required a leader to arise, and that leader was found in Sir William Wallace—a name that will be for ever dear to the Scottish heart.

In 1297 the insurrection became general. The Scots under Wallace defeated the English forces under the Earl of Surrey, and immediately afterwards the Scottish army ravaged Cumberland and Northumberland. Some of the Scottish soldiery pillaged and burned the priory of Hexham, and in retaliation Jedburgh Abbey was wrecked and plundered by the English under Sir Richard Hastings. The lead was stripped from the roof of the church, and the conventual buildings were so much destroyed that in 1300 the canons had to take refuge in other religious houses until their own was repaired. A writ is still extant ordering that Ingelram de Colonia be sent to the convent of Bridlington, in Yorkshire (*Beauties of Scotland*). On the King of England being petitioned by the abbot, the lead was ordered to be delivered up to him, but Sir Richard Hastings detained it for some time after that. It must have taken a considerable time to rebuild what had been cast down, and repair what was only partially destroyed; but as no portion of the conventual buildings has come down to our day, save a small piece of wall containing two arches near the south-west end of the church, we can form no idea of the character of the work. However, we may be sure that the chapter-house, refectory, scriptorium, and library, to say nothing of the other places requisite for a great abbey, would be in a style worthy of the abbey church.

The abbot of Jedburgh was one of the Scottish ambassadors to France in 1299, and while he and the others were returning, the King of England made arrangements to intercept them at sea. A sloop called *Our Lady of Rye* was manned and despatched, and letters were sent to the Goodman of Yarmouth and others enjoining them not to interfere with the master of the sloop, but to assist him in this affair (*Hist. Doc. Rel. to Scot.*, Vol. II.). It does not appear whether this attempt to intercept them was successful or not.

In vain did Edward I. attempt to crush the independence of Scotland as a nation, and to rule the country by means of his own officers. Mere force of arms could not accomplish this; nor had the execution of the heroic Wallace as a traitor on the scaffold at Smithfield any better effect. No sooner had the blood of this noble patriot been shed than it seems to have begun to flow in the veins of Bruce, by whose hand the banner of Scottish independence was again raised; and many were the writs issued by Edward II., who pursued the same policy as his father did regarding this country, ordering all churchmen, nobles, and others to obey the king's "custos" of Scotland, and to resist to the uttermost "Robertus de Bruce" and his accomplices (*Parliamentary Writs*). We learn from a writ, tested at Westminster on 13th December 1307, that Edward II., being on the point of setting out for the parts of France as far as Bologna for the settling of several special and arduous affairs touching his kingdom, caused a letter to be sent to the abbot of Jedburgh, affectionately requesting the said abbot that for the preservation of the peace of Scotland, and for the repelling of the hostile incursions of his rebels and enemies, he should exercise the same care and diligence that he had done hitherto, and for this service the king promised his special thanks on his return. Similar letters were sent to six Scottish bishops, nine Scottish abbots, and one prior (*Parl. Writs*, Vol. II., Div. II., p. 371).

In 1312-13 the Good Sir James Douglas, the staunch friend of Bruce, expelled the English from most of the strongholds on the Scottish Border; but even after Bannockburn Jedburgh Castle remained in the possession of the enemy, and continued to do so till after the battle of Lintalee, which took place about 1317.

William of Tynedale and other canons of the house of Gedworth, by their petition, having supplicated King Edward III. that since they and their abbot, exiled lately from Scotland and from the lands and tenements, &c., after the conflict at Stirling, because they were of English origin, he should grant a competent sustentation for themselves from lands, &c., the king committed to William of Ufton the custody of the lands and tenements, namely, of the manor of Lene (la Lene[1]) in Tynedale, and Torquen in Rydesdale, with their pertinents. Accordingly, from the proceeds of these lands he found twenty merks to each of these canons for their sustentation (Quoted from the *Originalia* in Hodgeson, Part III., Vol. II., p. 300).

The ambitious Edward Baliol, son of the late King John, had, in 1332, by the assistance of some interested English nobles, gained the crown of Scotland—which, however, he lost in a few months afterwards—and when he made a formal concession of the kingdom of Scotland and of his own private estates to Edward III. at Roxburgh, the abbot of Jedburgh, along with the abbots of Melrose, Dryburgh, and Kelso, was present. At the general peace in 1328, it was provided that the estates and revenues in England belonging to the abbeys of Jedburgh, Melrose, and Kelso should be restored to them. The orders given by the English king for this purpose in behalf of the monastery of Jedburgh were addressed to the "abbes de Pratis, near Northampton; the parson of Abbotslee,

---

[1] If Leam is meant, it lies on the Reed, near its junction with the Tyne below Bellingham. In the *Testa de Nevill*, Nicholas de Aketon held the greater Lem in Redesdale.

in Huntingdonshire; John de Bolynbroke, his own escheator; and Thomas de Featherstonhalgh" (Rymer, quoted by Morton).

Among the documents in the possession of Balliol College, Oxford, and noticed in the Fourth Report of the Royal Commission on Historical Manuscripts, is a confirmation in Latin, on parchment, by John, abbot of Jeddeworth, and the convent, in 1340, to Sir William de Felton, of a yearly payment of three merks, which he had been wont to receive from the church of Albotley (Abbotsley). From the same source we learn that the above William de Felton, knight, had the same year received from King Edward III. a grant of the advowson of the church of Abbotsley, which had come into the king's hands by the forfeiture of the abbot of Jeddeworth, with permission to the said William de Felton to give the same to the masters and scholars of Balliol, the statute of mortmain notwithstanding—which was by several other deeds accordingly done. The predecessors of John Rydel gave the advowson of the church of Adboldesle to the abbot of Geddeworth, with the tenth of the whole field of Adboldesle, of which land the foresaid church had hitherto been seized (Temp. Ed. I., *Rotuli Hundredorum*). Gervas Rydel, who afterwards became a canon of Jedburgh, and his brother, had given this church to the abbey. The hospital of St Mary Magdalene at Rutherford was granted to the monastery by Robert I., and after various changes the grant was confirmed by Robert III. in 1377. By the conditions of the grant the canons were obliged to maintain a properly qualified chaplain to celebrate divine service regularly in the chapel of the hospital, and who should pray for the king's soul, and for the souls of his ancestors and successors. In the event of the place being destroyed by war, the same services were to be performed in the monastery of Jedburgh by a chaplain till the hospital should be rebuilt (*Great Seal*). About 1444 this hospital seems to have been granted to one Alexander Brown.

REBUILDING OF THE NORTH TRANSEPT, CHOIR CHAPEL, AND TOWER.

DAVID II. of Scotland having refused to hold his kingdom in vassalage under Edward III. of England (the old claim having been revived), Scotland was subjected to another war, and at the battle of Neville's Cross, near Durham, in 1346, David was taken prisoner and carried to the Tower of London, and was not finally released from captivity for eleven years. A period of considerable prosperity for Scotland occurred between the liberation and death of David (1357 and 1371); and it may be that about that time, or shortly afterwards, the present north transept would be built. We know that in 1373 the canons were prosperous enough to be able to export wool, the produce of their own flocks; and the King of England in that year issued an order forbidding the collectors of his customs at Berwick to exact more than half a merk of duty on each sack of wool of the growth of Scotland, to the number of fourscore sacks, which should be exported by the abbots of Jedburgh, Melrose, Kelso, and Dryburgh. He also gave letters of protection, to continue for three years, in behalf of the abbots, monks, servants, and property of these monasteries (*Rotuli Scotiæ*). Notwithstanding these letters of protection, however, some of the canons who took a journey to England to sue for the restoration of property belonging to the churches annexed to their monasteries were barbarously murdered.

The style of the architecture of this part would quite agree with the period indicated, but there are other things to consider while attempting to fix the approximate date. The original transept was much shorter than the present one—all Norman transepts being short—and had there simply been a wish to lengthen it while entire, we should have expected that the end gable only would have been taken down and the new work added. Instead of this, we find that the west wall of the original transept has wholly disappeared, as well as a round pillar which stood at the end of the north aisle wall of the nave, and of two arches which it supported only a small portion of each remains at the side next the tower. The whole of this space is now occupied by an ugly dead wall. On the opposite side are seen the corresponding pillar and arches still entire, and immediately to the north of these are a nook-shaft and fragments of two arches, an upper and a lower, which seem to have been similar to those, still entire, in the south transept, where the stair leads up to the tower. On the outside is seen an entrance in the east wall which led from the triforium of the north chapel of the choir to a passage which no doubt went right round the original north transept, and a little further along, but higher up in the same wall, is what seems to have been the jamb of a window, with the spring of the arch still attached. The consideration of these facts would lead us to suppose that the old transept had been destroyed either by accident or as the result of war. We know of no accident that befell the abbey at that time to account for this destruction, and if it was brought about by war we must fix the date of the present transept a little later.

History records that Jedburgh Castle, having fallen into the hands of the English after the battle of Neville's Cross, remained in their possession for sixty-three years, until it was regained in 1409 by the people of Teviotdale, who razed it to the ground to prevent its ever again falling into the possession of the enemy.[1] In the following year Jedburgh was burned by the English under Sir Robert Umfraville, and again in 1416, the same being repeated in 1464 by the Earl of Warwick, but what injury was sustained by the abbey at these times we are not told. It is possible that the

---

[1] The fact that it was proposed to levy a tax of "two pennies" on every hearth in Scotland for the carrying out of its demolition, is sufficient to give some idea of the magnitude of the buildings. The money was, however, paid out of the national exchequer.

JEDBURGH ABBEY *from the* NORTH *in* 1877.

From a Photograph by Mr J. Hay Jedburgh.

transept may have been destroyed by Umfraville in 1410 or 1416, and that the Norman tower and south chapel were thrown down by Warwick in 1464, and this would satisfactorily account for the restorations. As has been stated, however, there is no historical proof that this was the case. That all these portions of the abbey were not rebuilt by the same workmen is all but certain, even by an examination of the masons' marks, those on the transept being quite different from those on the tower (see page of Masons' Marks).

The north transept is a fine specimen of Decorated work. The west wall is pierced with two pointed windows, each of which is divided by a mullion with a quatrefoil at the top. The sides of these windows are simply chamfered, or splayed, and the mullions also are plain. The great north window is divided by three mullions, which support beautiful tracery of a somewhat flowing character. The mullions here are moulded, and the sides of the windows are filled with mouldings much flattened and running into each other. A groove following the line of the gable-head is filled with the ballflower and other ornaments, and at the apex, immediately under the cross, is a beautiful representation of a human head. These, however, are modern, having been carved during the present century. There has evidently been some further alteration made at the same period near the top of this gable, as the wall recedes somewhat above the buttresses. It will also be observed that the top of the window arch does not exactly agree with the position of the shield above it. Jeffrey, in his *History of Roxburghshire*, says that the shield referred to originally bore the arms of the Kers. This statement is evidently incorrect. The stone is much defaced, but we can detect on the upper part of the shield the representation of a bishop's mitre, and in the lower part that of a fish similar to the one on the tomb of Archbishop Blackader in Glasgow Cathedral. The arms in all probability were those of one of the bishops of Glasgow, Jedburgh being in that diocese. The abbots of Jedburgh were not mitred abbots. This stone is probably not in its original place, and may have been built in there when the alterations alluded to were being made. No such stone appears in our old illustrations of 1775 and 1777. The transept is supported by buttresses placed at right angles, each of which is broken into stages, and terminates at the top of the wall with a slope longer than the other projections. On the face of one of the buttresses is a niche with a decorated corbel and canopy, but no statue now remains. Walcot, in his *Monasticon*, marks this as the sacristy, but on what authority we do not know.

In the north transept are interred many of the Kers of Ferniherst, valiant men, "wha keepit the marches in the days of auld." We learn from the Jedburgh Town Council Records, of date 1st February 1693, that Robert, Lord Jedburgh, one of the noble members of that house, by his testament, dated 4th November 1688, mortified a thousand pounds Scots, the interest of which was to be divided equally between the Grammar School and the poor of the parish ; and he also by the same testament mortified the sum of a thousand merks "for upholding the ylle [aisle] of Pherniherst." These two sums he ordained his nephew and executor, John Carre of Cavers, to pay and put into the hands of the Magistrates and Town Council for the purposes aforesaid. The minutes of Town Council of 2nd March 1706 set forth that "the said day it was represented by Walter Scot, provest, that my Lord Jedbrughes Ile, which the towne is obleidged to uphald wes lyke to become ruinous in severall places, and that necessar it is workmen be imployed to sight and repair the samyn. The Counsell appoynts Bailzie Olipher, Bailzie Elliot, the dein of gild, and thesaurer, to call tradesmen and view the said Ile, and wherein it is defective to caus repair the samyn immediatelie, and in the meintyme that the thesaurer provyd lyme." On the 11th of the same month the Town Council resolved to appoint the "commitie as befor to aggrie with workmen to repair my Lord Jedbrughes Ile, and to report that upon Wednesday nixt ; " and on the 16th the committee reported that they had agreed with Deacon Newton to repair the aisle for twenty merks, and that he "referes himselfe in the counsells will what more they will allow." The Council do not seem to have repaired the aisle or transept at any subsequent time, as the records are silent on the subject.

The south chapel of the choir is exceedingly interesting, as it shows a combination of two very different styles—the Early Norman and Second Pointed or Decorated. The window, which has two mullions with tracery—a quatrefoil and two pear-shaped openings —and nearly the whole of the wall, belong to the latter period. Here are two pretty corbels, one a representation of foliage, and the other of a human figure crushed down as if by carrying the weight of the groin. From these spring moulded ribs, which meet at the bosses the plain round ribs of the earlier period. At two of the bosses the different styles meet, and *go no farther*, but in one instance the round rib passes right across the groined roof from one old pillar to another, while the moulded rib which springs from the foliated corbel passes over to a pier of its own period. In this is seen an excellent example of how the work of restoration proceeded. As we have already remarked, whatever was left after the work of partial destruction was allowed to remain, if at all practicable, and hence it is that the new can always be distinguished from the old. The broken string-course in this chapel, the four arches (all imperfect in form) attached to the south-east pier of the tower, and other parts easily noticed throughout the building, sufficiently illustrate this. It is probable that this chapel and the south-east pier were restored by John Hall, who was appointed abbot on 10th December 1478,[1] and whose name is seen on the pier and on one of the bosses in the chapel. On another of the bosses is seen the lion rampant; and on the third one, from which a light seems to have been suspended, is seen the representation of four small human faces at the corners. The chapel is supported by two shelving buttresses, one

---

[1] Carta Johannis Hall, abbatis monasterii de Jedworth. Jacobus Dei gratia Rex Scotorum, omnibus probis hominibus suis, salutem. Sciatis nos venerabilem in Christo patrem Johannem Hall, in abbatem monasterii nostri de Jedworthe promotum, ad temporalitatem dicti monasterii ac omnium et singularum terrarum, redituum, ac possessionum, recepto prius ab eodem fidelitatis juramento, admisisse et eundem admittimus per presentes.—Apud Edinburgh, 10th December 1478 (*Register of the Great Seal*, General Register House, Edinburgh).

placed at right angles, and the other diagonally, a position frequently adopted in the later styles when buttresses were required at the quoins. On the former is a shield bearing a bull's head caboshed It has been stated that William Turnbull, bishop of Glasgow, "assisted in repairing the abbey of Jedburgh." Although we are not aware of the authority upon which this statement has been made, it is not unlikely to be correct, as Turnbull was a native of this district, and, as previously mentioned, Jedburgh was within the see of Glasgow. If it were true that he contributed towards the repair of the abbey, this would account for the presence of the bull's head—the crest of the Turnbulls—upon the buttress, but it must be stated that Bishop Turnbull died in 1454, at least twenty-four years before this chapel was rebuilt.[1] Jeffrey, in his *Roxburghshire* Vol. I., p. 288, says that it is very probable that Hall held the office for twenty-five years; but the following interesting entry, which we find in the *Acta Dominorum Concilii*, of date 3rd February 1484, shows this statement to be far from correct:—

"The lordis ordainis that lettres of our souuerain lordis be writin to command and charge Johne Rutherfurde, son to the lard of Rutherfurde, george of Newtoun, Adam ker, Jok Rutherfurde, Hob of Rutherfurde, John fawla, and all vther temporale men, our souuerain lordis liegis, being within the abbay and place of Jedworth, that thai in continent devoide and Red thaim furth of the said abbay, and suffre dene thomas cranstoun, abbot of the samyn, to enter therin efter the forme of the ordinaris lettres and our souuerain lordis admissioun, under the pain of Rebellioun and puttin of thaim to the horn, because their was generale comand diuerse tymes gevin of before be our souuerain lordis lettres that na temporale men suld remain in the said abbay nor hald the said dene

---

[1] Turnbull belonged to the Bedrule family. He was first a prebend of Glasgow, and afterwards Archdeacon of St Andrews, a Privy Councillor, and Keeper of the Privy Seal. He became Bishop of Glasgow in 1448, and afterwards he procured a Bull from the Pope for the erection of a college in that city. He died in Rome on 3rd September 1454 (Keith's *Catalogue of Scottish Bishops*). In Mrs Gordon's *Life of Sir David Brewster*, Turnbull is said to have founded and endowed the Grammar School of Jedburgh.

thomas furth of the samyn. And also that It be comandit of New be our said souuerain lordis lettres that zit as of before that na temporale men, our souueraine lordis liegis, in tyme to cum enter in the said abbay nor place of Jedworth, nor Remain therin, nor mak stoppin to the said dene thomas, abbot, to enter in the samyn as said Is, vnder the pain of Rebellioun forsayde, with Intimacion that quha sa dois in the contrar of this comand in tyme to cum that our souuerain lord wil in continent declare thaim his Rebells and put thaim to his horn, without ony vther processe or calling, bot alanerly that it be knawin that thai enter and Remain in the said abbay and place, And attoure because it is schewin and complenzeit to our souuerain lord that Adam ker, and certane vther temporale men, and also certane Religious men, put violent handis in his herrald and pursewand and wald hafe tane ther armes fra thaim, the lordis ordanis that the said Adam and the temporale men be summond til a certane day to ansuere to our souuerain lord apoun the said crime and offence, and also that lettres be writin to the bishop of glasgow ordinare charging him to call the Religious men that committit the said offence before him and punys thaim according to Justice."

The editor of *The Rutherfurds of that Ilk and their Cadets* (Edinburgh, 1884) points out that at this time the whole of the choir was already divided among the Rutherfurds for burying their dead, and he thinks a family quarrel had probably arisen in consequence of the abbot interfering to give some of the Cranstons place there. We do not know that there are any grounds for such a supposition.

It is evident that Cranston rebuilt the south-west pier of the tower, and part of the tower itself. The two north piers belong to the twelfth century, and the arch above, which is of the same date, is square-edged, while the arches of Cranston's time are chamfered. Cranston's initials, along with a representation of three cranes and two pastoral staves (sometimes, though erroneously, called crosiers), are seen on a shield on the pier built by him. His initials are seen also on the north side of the west arch, just where the chamfer begins; and the full name, "Abbas Thomas Cranstoun," appears at the spring of the south arch, immediately above the south-east pier. So anxious does Cranston seem to have been that posterity should have no difficulty in determining what work was done by him, that even a portion of the lower part of the north-west pier, which evidently he had repaired, bears his initials. The moulded base, which no doubt was put in by him, is quite different from the Norman base which adjoins it, and gives another of the many examples of the curious way in which the work of repairing or restoring was carried on. When Hall rebuilt the south-east pier he seems to have intended to throw an arch over to the south-west pier about half-way from the top, and the springer still remains to tell its story : but this idea not having found favour with Cranston, it was not carried into effect. Even the mouldings of Cranston's pier are different from those on that built by Hall. Fragments of the stone pavement are still seen at the bases of these piers. The tower, which would be restored a little before or about 1500, is very imposing, being 33 feet square and 86 feet high. There had been two floors. The upper storey, which, no doubt, was intended for a peal of bells, was lighted by narrow cusped windows on the east and west sides, while on the north and south sides there are openings for the emission of sound, and the top of the tower was arched over with stone. All around the top, immediately under the balustrade (which was restored in the early part of the present century), are numerous ornaments, many of which are grotesque representations of human heads. Near to the north-west corner is what has been represented to be the royal arms of Scotland, but which, upon examination through a glass, we found to be a shield surmounted by a cross, and bearing a chevron and three roses. On one side of the cross is the letter R, and on the other the letter B. We have ascertained the arms to be those of Robert Blackader,[1] bishop (afterwards arch-

---

[1] Robert Blackader, son of Sir Patrick Blackader of Tulliallan, was ninth bishop of Glasgow, and was translated to that see from Aberdeen in 1484. In addition to founding several altarages, he built some portions of Glasgow Cathedral. Blackader stood high in the confidence and favour of James IV., and was one of those who negotiated the marriage between that prince and the Lady Margaret of England, daughter of Henry VII. Spotiswood says that Blackader was succeeded by James Beaton in 1500 ; but this is an error, as he

bishop) of Glasgow, who was appointed to that see in 1484, and there is thus good reason to believe that this prelate had contributed towards the rebuilding of the tower. About half-way down the north side of the tower, and immediately under the centre opening, there is another shield with a chevron, and likewise surmounted by a cross. The arms and initials of the archbishop are seen also on a stone (not in its original place) built into the wall inside the north transept, under the great window.

---

held the see until his death in 1508. Cosmo Innes, in his *Lectures on Scotch Legal Antiquities*, p. 176, says that Glasgow became the see of an archbishop by papal grant in 1491; Hill Burton says that Glasgow was raised to an archbishopric in 1492; while Gordon states that Blackader was still bishop in 1507, and died archbishop in 1508. He had shortly before his death undertaken a pilgrimage to the Holy Land, and he died during the pilgrimage.

FURTHER VICISSITUDES: BURNING OF THE ABBEY BY THE ENGLISH.

AFTER the burning of the town by the Earl of Warwick in 1464, Jedburgh does not appear to have again suffered at the hands of the enemy for fifty-nine years; but in 1523—ten years after the battle of Flodden—both town and abbey suffered very severely by the English under the Earl of Surrey. On the evening of the 22nd of September, the enemy, to the number of 6000 fighting men, encamped on the south side of the Jed, and early next morning the town was stormed. The burghers, who could command no more than 1500 or 2000 men, made, nevertheless, a most determined resistance, and the English found it a hard task to become masters of the place. The abbey was also bravely defended, and although Surrey brought his cannon to bear upon it, it did not capitulate till two hours after nightfall. The monastery was then pillaged and committed to the flames, the effects of which are still visible on various parts of the ruins. Surrey's testimony to the valour of the Scottish Borderers at this time was, that he found them the boldest men and the hottest he ever saw in any nation.

It appears from a charter granted by John, abbot of Jedburgh, and the convent, on 23rd December 1541, and afterwards confirmed under the Great Seal, that William Douglas of Bonjedward had contributed towards the reparation of the monastery after this destruction, and that in return the said abbot and convent gave him in feu-farm the lands of Toftylaws and Paddohugh, in the barony of Houstoun (Ulston), which Douglas had held for nineteen years.

Robert Ker, son of Andrew Ker of Ferniherst, also contributed towards the restoration of the abbey about the same time, for which he received a charter from the abbot and convent on 7th June 1542 —confirmed under the Great Seal on 7th July—giving him in feu-farm the lands of Ancrum-Woodhead, &c., in Over Ancrum.[1]

Twenty years after Surrey's visit, Jedburgh seems to have recovered from the injuries it sustained under him, and Sir Ralph Eure, writing to the Earl of Hertford in March 1544, speaks of it as "the strength of Teviotdale, which, once destroyed, a small power would be sufficient to keep the Borders of Scotland in subjection." Hertford, writing to the King of England immediately afterwards on the same subject, said that he doubted not but "with the grace of God it should be feasible enough to win the town, and also the church or abbey, which was thought a house of some strength, and might be made a good fortress." The English Lords of Council having ordered Jedburgh to be taken if possible, and garrisoned if it could be made tenable, Lord Eure and his son, Sir Ralph Eure, Wardens of the East and Middle Marches, with all their forces, stormed the town on the morning of the 12th of June the same year, on which occasion the abbey was again pillaged and committed to the flames. Hertford,

---

[1] Apud Edinburgh, 7 Jul.—Rex confirmavit cartam Johannis Abbatis monasterii de Jedburgh, et ejusdem conventus, [qua pro nonnullis pecuniarum summis sibi persolutis, ac pro restauratione dicti monasterii per Anglos combusti et destructi, ad feodifirman dimiserunt Roberto Ker, filio secundo genito Andree K. de Farnyhirst, terras de Wodheid cum pendiculis, viz., *lie* Skaw-ward et Braidlaw in dominio de Ovir Ancrome, vic. Roxburgh, extenden. in rentali suo ad 20 marcas:—Tenend. dicto Rob. et heredibus masculis ejus de corpore legit. procreatis, quibus deficientibus, Joh. K. ejus fratri seniori et heredibus, &c. (*ut supra*) quibus def., legitimis et propinquioribus heredibus masc. dicti Rob. quibuscumque, arma et cognomen de Ker gerentibus, de dicto monast.— Reddend. annuatim 27 marcas, necnon astrictas multuras molendino dicti monasterii de Ovir Ancrome consuet.; et libertatem ad glebas effodiend. in *lie mos.* de Wodheid dictis abbati, &c., et *lie pleuch graith* in silva de W. aratris dicti monast. occupat., necessaria cum dictus Robertus et heredes ad hoc legitime requisiti forent., et heredes duplicando dict. firman at introitum suum; Test. Patricio Hepburn de Boltoun, Adam Kirktoun de Stewartfield, Georgio Moscrop burgen. de Jedburgh, Dominis Johanne Ker, Wil. Renkis, Jac. Jelien, Jacobo Simsorin, M. Waltero Pile, capellanis.—Apud dictum monasterium, 7 Jun. 1542.]—*Reg. Mag. Sig.*, Vol. III.

writing after this, says that Jedburgh was "well brent," and that after the assault it was "put to the fyre, and left not past two houses unbrent in the same; the abbey likewise they burned as much as they might for the stone work" (*Hamilton Papers*, Vol. II.). In the spring of 1545 Sir Ralph Eure occupied Jedburgh with an army of above 5000 men, with the intention of making it his headquarters until Teviotdale should be reduced to subjection to the King of England, but being that year defeated at Ancrum Moor, five miles from Jedburgh, where their leaders were slain, the English were once more compelled to cross the Border. The Earl of Hertford, with 12,000 men, entered Scotland in September that same year to avenge the defeat, and the effective way in which it was done may be learned from the fact that in this inroad were destroyed seven monasteries and friaries, sixteen castles, towers, and peels, five market towns, two hundred and forty-three villages, thirteen mills, and three hospitals. Jedburgh Abbey is in the list of places destroyed at this time. While this was being done on the Scottish Border, the Lords Home and Bothwell, with the abbots of Jedburgh and Dryburgh, assisted by a number of Frenchmen, made an incursion into Northumberland. In 1547, after the battle of Pinkie, the English placed several companies of Spanish soldiers at Jedburgh. Two years after this, the Scottish Government, afraid that it was intended to fortify the town, sent a body of French troops to retake it, and this was done without difficulty, as the Spaniards fled at the approach of the Frenchmen. Jedburgh was visited shortly afterwards by the Earl of Rutland, with 8000 men, at whose approach the French troops withdrew; but as the district was at that time quite destitute of provisions, the English soon returned to their own country.

EVENTS BETWEEN 1500 AND 1560.

THERE were stolen from the kirk of Jedburgh in 1502 certain "cusheis of silk," sheets, linen clothes, "fustiane," scarfs, and other clothes, and at the Justice aire in that year Robert Rutherfurde in Todlaw produced a remission for art and part of the theft (Pitcairn's *Criminal Trials*).

A respite, dated at Dumfries on 28th August 1504, was granted by James IV. under the Privy Seal, to a considerable number of persons, "men, kin, and tenants" of Archbishop Blackader of Glasgow, for the slaughter of Thomas Rutherfurd, committed in the monastery of Jedburgh (Pitcairn's *Criminal Trials*, Vol. II.). For the same slaughter, a remission, dated at Edinburgh, 28th February 1506, was also granted by the king to the same parties, including "John Foreman of Dawane, Baldred Blacater, knights; John Twedy of Drumelzear, Alan Stewart, Robert Blacater, son and apparent heir of Andrew Blacater of that Ilk; Adam Blacater, Charles Blacater, John Hergott, Adam Turnbull of Phillophauch, William Turnbull, his son and apparent heir; George Douglas of Bonjedburgh, John Douglas, his brother; Andrew Douglas in Tympanedene, Robert Douglas, his brother," and others (*Edgerston Papers*). The respite, published by Pitcairn, alludes to Archbishop Blackader as being "commendator" of the abbey. We have no particulars as to the cause or circumstances of this occurrence.

Some time after this William Rutherfurd of Longnewton was slaughtered in the abbey by Robert Ker of Newhall, but whether this was in any way connected with the other we are not aware. It is satisfactory, however, to know that this feud had a happy termination. In 1560 Ker of Newhall and the representative of the slaughtered man met at the kirk of Ancrum and there delivered up their swords as a token of amity, it being a further condition that one of the Kers should marry a Rutherfurd, and that another of the Rutherfurds should marry a Ker (*Edgerston Papers*).

Such inter-marriages were frequently resorted to with a view to settle family quarrels. An indenture was signed at Ancrum about the same time, designed to reconcile the Scotts and the Kers after the long feud between these two families, which had its rise at the skirmish near Melrose when Buccleuch attempted to rescue the youthful James V. from the Earl of Angus in 1526. One of the conditions of the indenture was that the heir of Buccleuch was to marry the sister of Ker of Cessford (Craig-Brown's *History of Selkirkshire*, Vol. I., pp. 150, 151).

In 1511, two years before the battle of Flodden, King James IV. granted extract from the register of a charter of King Robert the Bruce, under the hand of Gavin Dunbar, archdeacon of St Andrews, Clerk of the Rolls, in which charter King Robert confirmed to the abbot and convent of Jedburgh, the prior and canons of the same place abiding at Restennot, and serving God, keeping hospitality there, and their successors, the land of Restennot on which the church of Restennot was founded, Dunynad, Dissarth, and other lands in the county of Forfar in which they had been infeft by the king's predecessors, and in whose possession they were in the days of Alexander III., the king last deceased, as was manifest from an inquisition returned to the king's chapel. The charter then states that the charters and muniments of the said religious houses were lost and destroyed by wars and other fortuitous causes. This charter confirms, among other things, their right to 100 eels from the loch of Forfar; and also on the arrival of the king at Forfar, on any day whatever, two loaves of Sunday bread, four loaves of second bread, and six loaves of the kind called hugman's; also two stoups of the best ale; and two stoups of the small ale, called the kitchen ale (*Great Seal Register*, Vol. II.).

In 1516, when Lord Home and his brother William were condemned to death on a charge of intriguing against the Duke of Albany, then Regent, their brother, John Home, abbot of Jedburgh, was banished beyond the Tay, being believed to be implicated in their designs.

John Home, abbot of Jedburgh, was appointed clerk of expenses to the king in October 1526, as we learn from the following entry in the Privy Seal Register:—" Ane letter to Johne, abbot of Jedburgh, makand him clerk of expenses to our S[ouereign] L[ord] for all the dais of his lyfe, and gevand him all fies and dewiteis aucht thairof.—At Edinburgh, the last day of October 1526."

In October 1528 King James V. placed Lord Home and his brother, the abbot of Jedburgh, in Coldingham Priory, to keep it against the Earl of Angus; but Angus turned them out, and made it his residence for some time (*Douglas Book*, Vol. II., p. 173).

On 17th August 1539 a charter was granted in favour of the abbey of the lands of Aurchsook—alias Little Cossywnyn—in the county of Forfar, which lands had been held by John Lyoun, formerly Lord Glammys, and which fell to the king by the forfeiture of the said nobleman. This charter, along with others, was confirmed at Edinburgh under the Great Seal on 4th August 1542.

Pitcairn, in his *Criminal Trials*, gives an extract from the *Lord High Treasurer's Accounts*, of date 26th May 1541, showing that there was "gevin to the Gray Freris in Jedburcht, to the help of the reparatione of thair place, xx lbs;" and a parenthetical clause is inserted to explain that the place here meant was the monastery of Jedburgh. This, however, is incorrect. The place alluded to must be the convent of Grey Friars (Observantines) which was founded by the magistrates and inhabitants of Jedburgh in 1513. Of this convent nothing now remains.

In 1542 Andrew Ker of Ferniherst, Warden of the Middle Marches, received from King James V. a grant to himself and his heirs of the bailiary of the lands and lordship of Jedburgh Forest[1]

---

[1] Preceptum cartæ Andreæ Ker de farnyhirst, supra officio ballivatus totarum et integrarum terrarum et dominii de Jedburgh forest unacum advocatione donatione et jurepatronatus rectoriæ ecclesiæ de Sowdean, infra limites ejusdem quascunque, reddendo, &c.—Dated 2nd November 1542 (*Privy Seal Register*, Vol. XVI., folio 89B).

(which included the bailiary of the abbey); count, reckoning, and payment of the duties, &c., of the said lands to be made annually to the king and his exchequer. The office thus conferred remained in the family of Ferniherst for four generations.

Ten years after this there took place in the abbey what must have been one of the most imposing spectacles ever witnessed within its walls. David Panter, successively vicar of Carstairs, prior of St Mary's Isle in Galloway, and commendator of the abbey of Cambuskenneth, and who had been secretary to King James V. and the Regent Arran, was elected bishop of Ross in 1545. In 1552, on his return from France, where he had been residing as Scots ambassador for seven years, and "after he had rendered an account of his negotiations, and had received great thanks and applause for his good and wise management," he was consecrated with great solemnity in the abbey church of Jedburgh. In noticing this event, the splendour and dignity of which was enhanced by the presence of the Lord Governor, the flower of the Scottish nobility, and the leading Border chiefs, Bishop Lesly says that it was accompanied with great triumph and banqueting, and that the lairds of Cessford, Ferniherst, Cowdenknowes, Greenhead, Buccleuch, Littledean, and others received the honour of knighthood. If Buchanan's character of Bishop Panter, that he lived as if he had been trained not in the school of piety but of profligacy, or Knox's, that he died "eating and drinking, which, together with what thereupon depends, was the pastime of his life," be correct, the "banqueting" was probably of a kind not unworthy of record (Lesly's *History of Scotland;* Keith's *Scottish Bishops*, by Russell, p. 192; *John Knox's Works*, edited by David Laing, Vol. I., p. 263).

THE REFORMATION: SUPPRESSION OF THE MONASTERY.

> "All things have their end;
> Churches and cities, which have diseases like men,
> Must have like death that we have."

THE abbey seems to have suffered so severely in 1544-45 that it never recovered, and in 1559, like other monastic establishments throughout the country, it was suppressed. Various were the causes that led to the Reformation. Things might perhaps have gone on as they were for some time longer, had not the open traffic in indulgences aroused the wrath of Luther, who raised the spirit of the storm that sapped many of the bulwarks of Popery to their foundations. The springs were deep-seated; the waters struggled long to get to the surface; but when once fairly up, the flood of Protestant truth swept over Germany and the neighbouring countries of Denmark and Sweden, dashed along the mountain slopes of Switzerland, inundated Holland, and reached the shores of England and Scotland with such force that no human power could have stemmed the rushing tide. At the time of the Reformation there were about 260 conventual establishments in Scotland, and 4600 men and women are said to have been officially connected with them. Of these 13 were bishops, 60 abbots and priors, 500 parsons, 2000 vicars, and 1100 monks, friars, and nuns. Their wealth was enormous. Their lands, which were of great extent, were the richest and fairest in the country. It was therefore no wonder that there was a general scramble for possession when the crash came. The Reformed ministers wished to secure the property for the support of their church and the endowment of schools; but they had not sufficient influence to carry their wishes into effect. Previous to the suppression of the monasteries many of the nobility were made commendators of the great abbeys, and in not a few cases they were successful in retaining the property, though it was formally annexed to the Crown. The spirituality—that is, the teinds or tithes—of the Church were divided into thirds ; one-third was taken by the king, one-third was allowed to the old clergy, and the other third was given to the Reformed ministers. If the ministers got less than the third, as in many cases they did not get perhaps half of the third, the difference between the just third and what they actually got was called the superplus, and belonged to the king.

Not only was the Pope's jurisdiction and authority abolished in Scotland, and the temporalities of the kirk annexed to the Crown, but it was ordered that none say, hear, or be present at mass, under pain of confiscation of all their goods, and their persons to be in will for the first fault, banishment for the second, and death for the third. Another Act decreed that none go in pilgrimage to kirks, chapels, crosses, or the like, keep saints' days, sing carols, or observe any other superstitious papistical rite, under pain of "an hundred lbs. the landed man, an hundred merks the unlanded man, and 40 lbs. the yeoman; and offenders not responsal to be imprisoned for the first fault, and for the second that the offenders be punished by death as idolaters" (James VI., Parl. 7, cap. 104). But though there was this hatred to Popery and all that belonged to it, meet provision, as we have seen, was made for the support of the clergy who had belonged to the old faith.

Popery, however, was not easily put down, though abolished by the laws of the land, and the General Assembly was for a long time sorely exercised as to how it could be best extirpated. The Assembly supplicated the Lords of Secret Council for the due execution of the Acts of Parliament and Council against the Papists, and craved that the Exchequer might be the intromitters with the rents of those who were excommunicated, and that from the Exchequer the presbytery might receive the portion of the confiscated goods which the law appointed to be employed *ad pios usus*. Every presbytery was required to convene all known Papists within their bounds, and require them to put out of their company all friends and servants who were known to be Popish; also to give their children, sons and daughters, who were above seven years old, to be educated at their charges, by such of their Protestant friends as the presbytery should approve, and find caution for bringing home such of their children as were without the kingdom, to be educated in schools and colleges at the presbytery's sight. The presbyteries were further requested to see that these people found caution for their abstinence from mass, and that all, of whatever rank or degree, who refused to give satisfaction were to be proceeded against without delay. The commissioners of every presbytery were required to give in to the Assembly a list of the excommunicated Papists within their bounds, and of Papists' children out of the country, that the same might be presented by the Commissioners of Assembly to the Council; and all provincial synods, presbyteries, and kirk-sessions were to take particular notice of trafficking priests, and a list of their names to be given to the Privy Council. Ministers were to be at pains to dehort people from marrying with Papists, and hold forth the dangerous effects thereof (*Acts of Assembly*). "But still," says Hill Burton, "it [Popery] remained, lifting itself up in unexpected places, and frightening zealous Protestants, who felt like a settler in the wilderness when he believes that he has extirpated his venomous neighbours, yet beholds a viper gliding through the grass where his children are at play" (*Hist. Scot.*).

In 1562 the revenues of Jedburgh and those of Restennot and Canonby, dependencies of the abbey, were estimated at £1274, 10s. Scots money, two chalders and two bolls of wheat, twenty-three chalders of barley, and thirty-six chalders, thirteen bolls, one firlot, and one peck of meal, besides *cains* and customs (Keith's *History*, Ap. 185). The temporal possessions of the monastery at that time were the baronies of Ulston, Windington, Ancrum, Belses, Reperlaw, and Abbotrule. Its spirituality consisted in the kirks of Jedburgh, Eckford, Hownam, Oxnam, Longnewton, Dalmeny, Selbie, Wauchope, Castleton, Crailing, Nisbet, Spittal, Plenderleith, and Hopekirk. Of these, Selbie, Wauchope, and Castleton belonged properly to Canonby.

58 THE REFORMATION: SUPPRESSION OF THE MONASTERY.

To Restennot belonged the kirks of Forfar, Dounyvald, Aberlemno, and others. The priory of Restennot, which was situated in Forfarshire, was surrounded by a loch, and was accessible only by means of a causeway and drawbridge. The muniments and treasures belonging to Jedburgh Abbey were conveyed thither for safety in times of war with England. Walcott says its income was £275, 10s. 8d. During the sixteenth century the priory of Canonby was valued at £3, 8s. Prior to 1560, when certain sums were required for ecclesiastical purposes, it was taxed five different times. In the *Scotichronicon Abbreviatio* it is said that the priory of Blantyre, in Clydesdale, was a dependency of Jedburgh Abbey; but Spotiswood says it was a cell depending on Holyrood. It appears from a charter of confirmation granted by the king in 1575 that the abbot and convent of Jedburgh were at least patrons of Blantyre (*Great Seal*). In 1576 the third of the abbacy of Jedburgh was set down as £333, 6s. 8d.; wheat, eleven bolls, one firlot, and three pecks; bear, seven chalders, ten bolls, three firlots, and two pecks; and meal, twelve chalders, four bolls, one firlot, and three pecks; besides the third of the altarage of St Ninian. When a new order was issued in 1587 to collect the king's thirds of the benefices, Jedburgh was to pay £200, and Restennot £100.

Andrew Home, commendator of Jedburgh, sat in the Reformation Convention in 1560 (*Acta Parl.*).

Queen Mary appointed the 5th of November 1561 for the abbot to appear before her and the Privy Council for his interests in profit in Canonby (Armstrong's *Liddesdale*, p. 117).

In the queen's instructions to Lord James Murray, to be used by him in the Justice Court at Jedburgh on 15th November 1561, Andrew, commendator of Jedburgh, along with Sir Andrew Ker of Hirsel, David Turnbull of Wauchope, and others, were to appear at that court and answer for their diligence in apprehending "the faltours gevin in valentines [1] to thame" (*Privy Council Records*, 12th November 1561). Andrew, the commendator, was the second son

---

[1] In Scotland, sealed letters sent by royal authority to chieftains, landowners, &c., for the purpose of apprehending disorderly persons (Jamieson's *Scottish Dictionary*).

of George, fourth Lord Home, and brother of Alexander, the fifth lord, who was father of the first earl. Mr Morton, on the authority of Wood's *Peerage*, says that Andrew was son of George, fourth Earl of Home; and Nisbet says he was son of the third Lord Home. In a charter in favour of William Scott of Haughhead, dated 30th June 1588, and also in a precept of *clare constat*, dated 20th August 1594, in favour of Mark Scott, son of the said William Scott, deceased, Andrew, the commendator, styles himself " frater germanus quondam Alexandri Domini Home." This umquhile lord must have been Alexander, fifth baron, son and heir of George, fourth baron, who died in 1575. Foreseeing that the abolition of his abbey was imminent, the commendator, like the abbots and commendators of similar establishments, made over the lands, &c., belonging to the monastery to his chief, or rather to his own mother, who was the widow of George, fourth Lord Home, and on the death of Lady Home he made a new grant of the lands of the abbey in favour of his nephew Alexander, Lord Home, who was infeft in them in 1564. On the death of Lord Home in 1575, his son Alexander, the sixth lord, obtained a precept from the commendator for infefting him as heir to his father in 1587.

On 23rd March 1579-80, Andrew, "permissione divina commendatarius perpetuus monasterii de Jedburgh," and the convent, granted a charter of feu-farm to Alexander Hume of Huttonhall of the three corn-mills and the waulk-mill belonging to the monastery, he paying for the same annually, for the three cornmills the sum of £90, 10s. Scots, and for the waulk or fulling mill the sum of £5, 10s. Scots, being the old rent in use to be paid for the same. This was confirmed by Crown charter of date 26th May 1587.

On 30th June 1588 the commendator granted letters of tack and assedation, dated at the abbey of Jedburgh, to William Scott in Haughhead of the teind sheaves of the town and lands of Haughhead with their pertinents, lying within the barony of Eckford, for ten years from that date, " payand thairfoir zeirlie the said William Scott, his airis and assignayis, to ws and our successors, commendators of the said abbey, our factoris and chalmerlainis in our name the sowme of thrie bollis beir, and fywe bollis straikkit meill, gud and sufficient mercat stuff, betuix the feistis of Sanctandrois day and candilmes allanerlie, and delyuering the samen within our girnell in the said abbey as vse is, or to sik personis as we sall assigne to uplyft the same." To this document was appended the common seal of the chapter, and Andrew Clayhills, minister of Jedburgh, was one of the witnesses.

A dispute having arisen with regard to the right of certain parties to the monks' portion, superplus, and temporalities of the abbacy, the question was brought before the Lords of Session, who found that the matter arose out of the multitude of Acts made anent the same, and annexing the same to the Crown; and in 1593 the Scottish Parliament passed an Act reponing to Andrew, the commendator, his own right of the temporalities during his own lifetime, as if the same had never been taken from him.

By the Act of General Revocation, 29th July 1587, the bailiary of the abbey lands, an office which had been held by the Kers of Ferniherst since 1542, was, along with the temporalities of the abbey, annexed to the Crown; but in the following year Sir Andrew Ker of Ferniherst was by a Crown charter confirmed in his "native possession" of the bailiary of all the lands, lordships, and baronies belonging to the abbey, wherever lying within the county of Roxburgh, to be held by him and his heirs on payment of a blench duty of one penny yearly.[1]

---

[1] Sciatis nos intelligentes per autentica documenta quod quondam Andreas Ker de pharnyhirst, [quondam Johannes Ker de pharnyhirst], et quondam Thomas Ker de pharnyhirst, milites, proavus, avus, et pater dilecti nostri Andreæ Ker, nunc de pharnyhirst, legitime constituti fuerant ballivi omnium terrarum, dominiorum, et baroniarum monasterio nostro de Jedburgh pertinentium, ubicunque jacentium infra vicecomitatum nostrum de Roxburgh .... volentes dictum Andream et hæredes minime lædi aut præjudicari in sua nativa possessione officii dedisse, concessisse hereditarie et hac præsenti carta nostra confirmasse dicto Andreæ Ker, heredibus suis, &c.—Dated at Holyrood House, 15th March 1587-88 (*Great Seal Register*, Lib. 37, No. 118).

The words in brackets, which are not found in the charter as recorded,

THE REFORMATION: SUPPRESSION OF THE MONASTERY. 61

In 1600 an Act was passed in favour of Alexander Lord Home anent the thirds of Coldingham and Jedburgh. The Act sets forth that "because the tyme of the first upgiving of the rents, the same were in the auld integritie, and were able to pay the auld assumit third thereof, whilk they are not now able to beir, his provision thereof being nae forder extended but the spirituality of the same, whilk for the maist pairt is set in lang takis, great pensions gevin furth of the samyn, mony monk's portions evictit furth thereof, and the hail temporalities annexed to the Crown, wherethrough Lord Home and the ministrie are defraudit of the payment of the sure third which the rents are not able to beir." A new "just third" was therefore ordered to be made.

About the time that Lord Home was created an earl he resigned into the hands of the king the lands of the abbey, and obtained a re-grant of them by Crown charter of date 10th May 1606. In that year the abbacy, along with the priories of Canonby and Coldingham, was erected into a barony, called the Barony of Coldingham, and granted to the Earl of Home, whose minor dignities were Lord Jedburgh and Dunglas; and the priory of Restennot was also erected into a barony in favour of Viscount Fentoun. From the grant to the Earl of Home were excepted the kirk of Dalmeny, which belonged to Jedburgh, and the right of patronage of that kirk, which had been given to Sir Thomas Hamilton of Binning; and the kirk of Lavertoune, and certain lands, &c., which had belonged to Coldingham, and were now given to the Earl of Dunbar. There was granted the same year to Preston of Pennycuik a pension of £300 from the abbacy of Jedburgh, which was ratified by Act of Parliament in 1641.

On 26th February 1606 Sir John Ker of Hirsel obtained a

---

are here supplied from the precept of the charter in the Privy Seal Register (Lib. 57, folio 52B). Further on in the charter, and also in the precept, the lands are described as lying "infra dictum nostrum vicecomitatum de *Jedburgh*."

As no profit was derived from the office of bailie of the monastery, the Marquess of Lothian did not put in any claim at the abolition of the heritable jurisdiction (Chalmers' *Caledonia*).

Crown charter giving him the mills of Jedburgh which had belonged to the abbey.

In 1610 another charter of the lands and lordship of Jedburgh was granted under the Great Seal in favour of the Earl of Home, and in the following year there was a contract of excambion, dated "At Edinburgh, and Coldingknows, Jedburgh, the sext, twenty, and twenty thrie days of Junii, Julii, respective, 1611, (by which) it is appointit, agreit, and finallie contractit betwix ane nobill and potent Erll Alexandre Earl of Home, Lord Jedburgh and Dunglas, and Sir John Ker of Hirsell, kng$^{t.,}$ heritable feuar of the Landis, mylnes, fishings, &c., and utheris aftermentionit, with express avyse and consent of Dame Margaret Quhitlawe, his spous, for all richt, titill, entress, and clame of richt quhilkis sche had, hes, or ony wayis may clame or have to the samin landis, teyndis, mylnes, and utheris efter-specifet, with thare pertinentis, be conjunct fie, lyfrent, terce, or be quhatsumever either manner of way; and siclyke the saide Schir Johne takand the burden upone him, and his airies for hir, (sells and dispones) to the saide Nobill Erle and his airis maill, and assignees quhatsumever, heritablie and irredimable, all and sindri the Lands of Hirsell, with towere, fortalice, manor-place, mylnes, &c. And to that effect the saide Schir Johne be thir presentis, binds and oblissies him and his airis, &c., to infeft dewlie and sufficientlie be charter, and seasing, the said Nobill Earle and his airis male and assignais forsaidis (in the above Landis), and to mak seil, subscryve, and deliver to thame charter contening precept of Seasing, and procuratorie of Resignatione zerupone in sic due and competent forme as effeiris." The only burdens affecting the lands were a wadset of the "Est manis of Hirsel" to Sir John of Huttonhall, and Samuel Home, his brother, the right of redemption of which was assigned to the earl, and localities in favour of the dowagers of the family, which were specially exempted. In exchange the earl disponed the lands of Jedburgh to Sir John Ker, which he immediately afterwards possessed, and thereby was designated.

The Kers of Hirsel were a younger branch of the Cessford family. Mark Ker of Littledean, second son of Walter Ker of

Cessford, obtained the lands of Dolphingston by marriage with Marjory Ainslie, Lady of Dolphingston, and in 1542 their son, Sir Andrew Ker, afterwards designed of Dolphingston, of Littledean, and of Hirsel, received from James V. a grant of "the king's lands of Hirsel." It was by the grandson of this Sir Andrew that these lands were excambed for those of Jedburgh, as stated above. Hume of Godscroft says that Ker got the Hirsel on account of his being the first to bring to the king tidings of the victory won by the Lords Home and Huntley over the English at Haddonridge.

After obtaining possession of the lands and lordship of Jedburgh, Sir John Ker, as above mentioned, assumed the territorial designation "of Jedburgh." In an instrument of sasine dated 1st April 1613, two years after the excambion, and proceeding on a feu-charter granted by Sir John in favour of Walter Turnbull of Rawflat, in the lands of Rawflat and Ryknowe in the barony of Belses, and of Nether Bonchester and Braidhaugh in the barony of Abbotrule, he is designed as "de Jedburgh"—"nunc hereditarius feudifirmarius terrarum et dominii de Jedburgh."

In consequence of difficulties having occurred as to Sir John's right to the territorial lordship of Jedburgh, including the abbey, several transactions were entered into between him and the Home family for the purpose of having his feudal title completed, and in 1619 he obtained a charter from the Crown. The same year, Walter, first Earl of Buccleuch, purchased from Sir John the lands of Boxtonleys, Chiefthope, Over and Nether Whitkirk, Whiland, Ormiscleuch, Abbotsyke, and Abbotshaws, all of which lands had in former days belonged to the abbey of Jedburgh. He also at the same time purchased the teinds of Castleton and Erkleton, and all other lands belonging to the old cell of Canonby (*Scotts of Buccleuch*, Vol. I., p. 252). As part of the excambion arrangement, the Earl of Home promised to obtain an Act of Parliament dissolving the abbey from the Crown, and to resign the abbey for a re-grant by the Crown to Sir John Ker; but Lord Home having died before these promises were fulfilled, a new contract was entered into with his successor in 1621 to carry out the arrangement of 1611. Sir

David Home of Wedderburn was provided to the abbacy, which was held to be vacant by the decease of Earl Alexander. In 1621 Sir David, with consent of the convent, made resignation and demission of the same to the king in order that it might be granted to James, Earl of Home, which was accordingly done the same year by Act of Parliament, followed by a Crown charter, erecting the lands of the abbey and those of Canonby into a free barony, called the Barony of Jedburgh, in favour of Lord Home. The same year Parliament ordained that no ratification of the abbacy, or any part thereof, be expede in favour of Sir John Ker until he found caution to settle the Laird of Ferniherst in his teinds of Ferniherst, Oxnam, Hobkirk, Fewrewll [Bedrule?], Over and Nether Wells, Over Crailing, Swinside, the said laird having to pay to Sir John some reasonable duty, and to the ministers serving kirks where these lands were situate, and likewise some reasonable duty *pro rata* according to the modification that was already made or should be made for stipends to the same. On a new resignation by the Earl of Home, Sir John's title to the barony of Jedburgh was completed by a Crown charter.

In 1622 Sir Andrew Ker of Ferniherst was created Baron Jedburgh. Some have stated that along with the title he received the lands and barony of Jedburgh; but this is not correct, as they were still in possession of Sir John Ker.

Some time after Sir John got possession of the lands of the abbey he appears to have become embarrassed in his pecuniary affairs, and Sir Thomas Hamilton, king's advocate—familiarly known as "Tam o' the Cowgate"—who had been created Earl of Melrose,[1] a title afterwards changed for that of Haddington, apprised the lands and lordship of Jedburgh from Sir John Ker for payment of £5837, 10s. Scots; and in 1623 the Earl of Melrose obtained a Crown charter of the lordship of Jedburgh. He afterwards assigned his right to Jedburgh in favour of his son Thomas, Lord Binning,

---

[1] "A title which, after bearing it eight years, he relinquished for that of Haddington, thinking, it is said, a title derived from a county more honourable than one from an abbey" (*Historical Account of the Senators of the College of Justice*, p. 223).

who led a new apprising against Sir John Ker for £17,333, 6s. 8d. Scots, and on that apprising obtained a charter from the Crown in 1624. In 1632 John Ker of Langnewton and Littledean, as son and heir of Sir John Ker of Jedburgh, then deceased, ratified in favour of Thomas, Lord Binning, his apprising of the lands, lordship, and barony of Jedburgh. Lord Binning held the property till the year 1637, when, after succeeding his father as second Earl of Haddington, he sold and disponed to William, the third Earl of Lothian, the lands, lordship, and barony of Jedburgh, a transaction which was ratified by Act of Parliament in 1641. It would seem that Robert, second Earl of Lothian, who was father-in-law of William, third Earl —the latter having married the second earl's eldest daughter Anna, Countess of Lothian—had also acquired a certain interest in the lordship and barony of Jedburgh as a creditor of Sir John Ker of Jedburgh. The second Earl of Lothian's two daughters, the Ladies Anne and Joanna, were served heiresses to him, each in one-half of the lordship of Jedburgh. These retours were expede in 1642, and on the resignations made by Thomas, Earl of Haddington, and the two co-heiresses of Robert, second Earl of Lothian, William, the third earl, obtained a Crown charter on 5th March 1642, which completed his title; and from that date to the present time the lordship of Jedburgh has continued the property of the Lothian family. William, the third Earl of Lothian, was third in descent from Robert, third son of Sir Andrew Ker of Ferniherst, and this Robert was uncle to Sir Thomas Ker of Ferniherst, the zealous champion of Queen Mary.

We have now completed our survey of the rise and fall of this monastic establishment. From the time of David I., who founded the abbey, till the Reformation, when it was suppressed, four hundred years had elapsed, and that period had proved an eventful one for Scotland. The national prosperity, as we have seen, received a severe check after the death of Alexander III., from which it did not fully recover for several centuries. The independence of the country, which had been endangered by the ambition of the English kings, was, after being gallantly defended by Wallace, permanently established by Bruce on the field of Bannockburn. But the two countries waged war with each other for centuries with only brief intervals of peace; and Scotland suffered severely from this cause, as well as from the almost constant feuds of her own nobles.

It was, as we have previously said, only in the seclusion of the cloister or cell that, at the period when these buildings were erected, religion found her home, and that the arts and sciences flourished under the fostering care of the monks, so that the monasteries, raised by pious hands for the most worthy of all objects, and endowed by a wonderful liberality, long exercised a beneficial and powerful influence upon society. But those great and once potent institutions were not exempt from the mighty law of change; and though they had, during a certain period of their existence, proved of importance in preserving something like a living Christianity, they were in time suppressed, and the remains of their once extensive buildings—now silent witnesses of the past—serve only as interesting objects to the student of architecture or to the ordinary tourist.

> "The sacred tapers' lights are gone,
> Grey moss has clad the altar stone,
> The holy image is o'erthrown:
>   The bell has ceased to toll."

THE ALTARAGES IN THE ABBEY.

Of the altarages in the abbey very little is known. The earliest notice we have met with is in a charter granted to the chaplains in the church of Jedworth, dated at Jedworth on 30th August 1479, and confirmed under the Great Seal on 21st November of the same year (*Great Seal Register*, Lib. 9, No. 13).

In the charter referred to, Mr James de Newton, "rector ecclesiæ parochialis de Bothroule" (Bedrule), grants ten merks yearly from two tenements belonging to him in Jedworth to Walter Henrison and his successors, chaplains at the altar of St Kentigern (St Mungo),[1] in the church of Jedworth.[2] After the death of the granter, the patronage of the said chaplainry and altar was to devolve upon James Rutherford of that Ilk and his heirs, and presentation to be made within twenty days, failing which the provost, bailies, and community of Jedworth were to present within eight days. The chaplain was to perform daily service at the altar in praise of the omnipotent God and His Mother the Virgin Mary, and for the salvation of the souls of James II., King of Scots, James III., King of Scots, and Margaret, Queen of Scots, his spouse; and for the salvation of the souls of the donor, of his father, of his mother, and of all his predecessors and successors, and of all the departed faithful.[3]

---

[1] St Kentigern was called in the language of the ancient Britons Munghee, or Mungho, "one dearly beloved" (Alban Butler's *Lives of the Saints*).

[2] This charter is referred to by David Laing in his edition of *Robert Henryson's Poems*, p. xxxix., Edinburgh, 1865.

[3] In "A Perfect Inventor of all the Donations since the days of King Ja : the ffirst to the reigne of King James the 6th inclusive as also thereafter" (*MS. Volume in Stirling's and Glasgow Library*), there is mention of a "C. of con-

We find reference to two other altarages in a charter granted by James VI. to the provost, bailies, council, and community of Jedburgh, dated at Edinburgh, 24th November 1569 (*ibid.*, Lib. 32, No. 87). The charter sets forth that, with a view to provide for the preaching of the Word of God, and for the hospitality and assistance of the poor, the maimed, the wretched, the impotent, and orphans within the burgh, the king gave all lands, tenements, annual rents, acres, crofts, profits, dues, and emoluments whatsoever that belonged to the chaplainries or altarages of the Blessed Mary and of the Holy Rood, situated and founded in the parochial church of Jedburgh, and which were possessed and uplifted by the last chaplain and possessors of the same respectively, namely, umquhile Dominus John Wood, last chaplain of the altarage of the Blessed Mary, and umquhile Master Walter Pyle, last chaplain of the altarage of the Holy Rood, within the church aforesaid, and then vacant by their decease; likewise all other chaplainries, altarages, or chapels, in whatever church founded within the liberty and parish of the said burgh of Jedburgh, and then vacant, or that might in future happen to become vacant, by whatsoever patron founded. After reciting that great fraud had been practised by no small number of the chaplains and prebendaries, who after the reformation of religion disponed, alienated, and away gave the lands, tenements, and annual rents, mortified to their altarages and chaplainries, into the hands of private persons, the charter rescinds and annuls all such transactions by which the first will and intention of the founder was changed. Nevertheless, the will of the king was that whatever chaplains, possessors of the said altarages or chaplainries, were remaining and had provision from the same before the Reformation, should by no means be prejudiced by this infeftment, but should enjoy the said fruits and dues during their life only.

---

firmation of a mortification maid be Mr James Newtoun, parsone of Bothwell, to a chaplane at St Mungoes altar in Jedburgh of ten merks of annual rent zeirely out of his two tenements in Jedburgh, particularly described therein dated 4 Nov^{r.}, 1479." The "Bothwell" here is evidently a mistake for "Bothroule"—Bedrule.

In 1498, Robert Ker of Sonderlandhall sold his lands of Esselieband to Sir William Douglas for 240 merks Scots, to be paid "on one day between sunrise and sunset in the parish church of Jedworcht, upon the altar of St Mary the Virgin" (*History of Selkirkshire*, by Mr Craig-Brown, Vol. II.).

The Town Council, on 30th January 1664, appointed James M'Cubbie and William Brown, bailies, to speak with the late provost anent the "alterag" contained in the town's charter. On 13th February following, a committee was appointed to take one of the old registers to revise the same anent anything that could be found concerning the altarage.

In addition to the altarages we have named there was an altar in the abbey dedicated to St Ninian. On 11th October 1503, at the altar of St Ninian, there was drawn up a notarial instrument on the consignation of Mr Gawin Douglas, provost of St Giles College Church, Edinburgh, as procurator for George, Master of Angus, Lord of Jedworth Forest, into the hands of David Douglas, burgess of Jedworth, of the sum of 100 merks Scots, to be kept for the profit of Ralph Ker of Primsydloch, to whom the said Gawin had offered it for the redemption of the lands of Langlee and Gillistungis, in the lordship of Jedworth Forest, but who would not resign the said lands, in respect that, as he thought, the seven years' tack of the lands which he offered him, in terms of the letters of revision, was not sufficient. Among others present were Walter Scot of Buccleuch, knight, William Ker of Zare, and George Douglas of Bonjedworth (*Douglas Book*, Vol. III., pp. 180, 181). In 1576, when an account was taken of the thirds of benefices, the third of the altarage of St Ninian in Jedburgh was £3, 4s. 5d.

THE SEAL OF THE CHAPTER OF JEDBURGH.

SEVERAL impressions of the common seal of the abbey, as well as of the office of abbot of Jedburgh, are still in existence.

Mr Henry Laing, in his volume of the *Ancient Seals of Scotland*, figures and describes two seals which had belonged to the abbot's office, as also the common seal of the chapter. The first is appended to a convention between the abbots of Melrose and Kelso regarding the lands of Bouldin, Eldon, and Dernewick, A.D. 1220. This—probably the first seal that belonged to the office—is described as representing a female figure sitting before a lectern, on which is a book, which she holds open with her left hand; her right hand holds a crosier, and her head is inclined upwards, as if engaged in singing praises. The legend is: [S]IGILLVM : COM : ABB[ATIS : D]E : GEDDEW[ORTHE].

Another of the seals is appended to a gift to Alexander Lyon, chanter of Moray, of the non-entry of the lands of Cossin or Ardquhork, in Forfar, part of the ancient patrimony of Restennot, 1532. It represents, beneath a Gothic canopy, the flight of the Holy Family into Egypt; and in the lower part is the figure of a monk kneeling at prayer, with the legend: S : OFFICII : ABBATIS : MON : DE : JEDWORT.

The common seal of the chapter, as appended to the sasine of the lands of Cossins, 1534, is described in the same work as representing the Father crowning Mary within a niche, while on the counter seal is a representation of the salutation of the Virgin. The impression, the author states, is in bad preservation, which no doubt accounts for the reading he gives of the legend. The same seal, but without the reverse, is attached to the grant by the abbot and convent to William de Felton, noticed on page 38 as being among the documents in Balliol College, Oxford; but this is also much defaced. We have had in our possession, the property of the late Mr John Crosby, Glasgow, a beautiful and almost perfect impression of this seal, which shows that the legend on the obverse is: SIGILLVM : COMMVNE : CAPITVLI : DE : IEDDEWORTHE; but that on the counter seal which Henry Laing has deciphered as MATER : CASO . . . . SERVIS . . . . ANIA : should be + MATER : CASTA : [PI]A : SERVIS : SVCCVRRE : MARIA. It is appended to letters of tack and assedation, dated 30th June 1588, from Andrew, commendator of Jedburgh, to William Scott, of the teind sheaves of the town and lands of Haughhead, afterwards noticed.

The two illegible letters are supplied as above on the suggestion of Thomas Dickson, LL.D., Curator of the Historical Department, General Register House, Edinburgh. His reading is all the more probable from its giving a rhyming hexameter, and may be fortified by the closing words of the " Salve Regina " in the Rosary or Virgin's Psalter ordered by Pope Pius V.: " O clemens, O pia, O dulcis Virgo Maria ; " or, in the English version :—

"O merciful, O pious Maid,
O gracious Mary, lend thine aid."

The abbots' personal seals, so far as they are known, will be described in treating of the Superiors of the Monastery.

SUPERIORS OF THE MONASTERY.

OF the superiors of the monastery very little is known; even a few of the names may be lost. We have here attempted to make a list of them, and have noted what could be gathered concerning each. It will be found that our list is by far the most complete that has hitherto been published.

DANIEL was prior in 1139, as appears from a charter of that year by David I. to the monastery of Coldingham.

OSBERT, who was first a prior, and afterwards raised to the dignity of an abbot, is said to have been a man of singular piety, and to have written a treatise to the king concerning the founding of the monastery. He composed the rules and registered the acts of the chapter. As prior he witnessed a grant by David I. to St Mary's Church, Stirling, in 1147, and as abbot he witnessed a charter of confirmation to the abbey of Kelso by Malcolm IV. in 1159. In 1160 and 1163 Osbert witnessed grants to Cambuskenneth Abbey, which is only another name for St Mary's Church, Stirling. He died in 1174, and is alluded to in the *Melrose Chronicle* as "primus abbas de Jeddeworthe."

RICHARD, the cellarer of the abbey, next succeeded to the office, and died in 1192.

RALPH, one of the canons, who succeeded on 29th May the same year, was reputed to be a seer. He died on 7th August 1205, much regretted by his brethren.

HUGH, who was previously prior of Restennot, was next abbot of Jedburgh. This abbot attested a document defining the boundaries between the grounds of Eildon and Bowden, to prevent quarrels in future between the monks of Melrose and Kelso (*Cart. Mel.* and *Harl. MS.*, 3960, fol. 41R.). Laing gives a seal of Hugh, bearing a figure of the abbot, in cowl, holding his staff, seated on a carved chair in profile to the right, reading a book upon a carved lectern. Legend: [S]IGILL : HVGON[IS] : ABB[ATIS : D]E : GEDEW . . . . (*circa* 1220).

PETER held office from 1220 till at least 1226. Mr Bruce Armstrong, in his *History of Liddesdale, &c.*, pp. 107-10, refers to a dispute between Walter, bishop of Glasgow, and Peter, abbot of Jedburgh, in 1220, regarding the priory of Canonby and the church. He is mentioned in the chartulary of Dryburgh Abbey as abbot in 1226.

HENRY. All that is known of this abbot is that he resigned his charge on account of his great age and infirmities in 1239. He was succeeded by

PHILIP, previously one of the canons, who was abbot ten years. He sat with the king in council in 1244 (*Acta Parl. Scot.*, Vol. I.). He died in 1249 (*Extracta ex Chronicis Scotiæ* and *Melrose Chronicle*).

ROBERT DE GYSBORNE, another of the canons, was next elected to the office of abbot, but died the same year. We are told that the very appearance of this abbot inspired devotion. He was succeeded by

NICHOLAS DE PRENDERLATHE, another of the canons, the same year. At Roxburgh, on 20th September 1255, he was, along with many others, admitted into the King's Council for the management of certain matters on the Borders. In the same year he, along with other magnates of the king, recommended the removal of the bishops of Glasgow and Dunblane and others from the King's Council and their office, in consequence of their demerits, and recommended that others should be appointed of his council, and regents of the kingdom, and guardians of the king and queen (*Cal. of Doc. Rel. to Scot.*, Vol. I.). In 1256 the king, on the recommendation of his envoys, including Abbot Nicholas, convened a parliament to be held in Stirling (*ibid.*, Vol. I.). This abbot, along with the bishop of Dunblane and the abbot of Melrose, performed the ceremony of excommunication against the councillors of the king in the abbey of Cambuskenneth in 1257 (*Melrose Chronicle*, p. 182). In 1265 he was, along with three other persons, sent on a mission from King Alexander III. to Henry III. of England, at that time in custody of the Earl of Leicester, whose prisoner he had been since the battle of Lewes the preceding year. He retired in 1275 in consequence of old age. He was a man of wisdom and prudence.

JOHN MOREL, who was also chosen from among the canons, was abbot when Alexander III. was married in the abbey in 1285. He was one of the three commissioners sent by the Scottish Parliament to the English king anent the rival claims of Bruce and Baliol to the throne of Scotland. He sat in the convention at Brigham on 14th March 1289-90. In 1290 he concurred in a letter of the Commonwealth of Scotland to the King of England approving of the proposed marriage of the king's son with Margaret of Norway, the heiress of the Scottish crown. In December 1292 he was present at Newcastle when Baliol acknowledged King Edward to be his feudal superior. He swore fealty to King Edward at Berwick on 2nd September 1296. His retirement was reported to the king the same month. Mr Henry Laing, in his *Catalogue of Scottish Seals*, describes this abbot's seal as a very neat one, having the device of a horse, and, in the upper part, a small figure having the appearance of a gauntlet, all surrounded by a border of plain tracery. Legend: S : FRATRIS : JOHANNIS : MOREL. A.D. 1292.—Chapter House, Westminster.

WILLIAM DE JARUM, the prior, was next elected abbot. The election took place by permission of Edward I. of England, as appears from the following writ entered on the Patent Rolls of the year m. 6. 1296 :—

"Fratres Willelmus de Jarum, Petrus Gernoun, et Johannes de Tyttyntone, canonici de Jeddeworthe, nunciantes regi cessionem fratris

Johannis nuper abbatis ejusdem, loci, habent litteras regis de licentia eligendi.

"Teste rege apud Berewyke super Twedam, xiij die Septembris."

De Assensu Electioni Adhibito.

"Rex venerabili in Christo patri eadem gratia Glasguensi episcopo, salutem. Sciatis quod electioni nuper factæ in ecclesia conventuali de Jeddeworthe de fratre Willemo de Jarum, priore ejusdem domus, in abbatem illius loci, regium assensum adhibuimus et favorem. Et hoc vobis tenore præsentium significamus, ut quod vestrum est in hac parte exequamini. In cujus, &c.

"Teste rege apud Alnewyke, xxiij die Septembris."

"Pro priore de Jeddeworth de temporalibus abbatiæ prædictæ per Johannem de Warrena, &c., custodem regni et terræ Scotiæ, eidem 'priori' nomine regis deliberandis.

"Rex dilecto et fideli suo, Johanni de Warenna, comiti Surriæ, custodi suo regni et terræ Scotiæ, salutem. Cum nos electioni nuper factæ in ecclesia conventuali de Jeddeworthe de fratre Willelmo de Jarum, priore ejusdem domus, in abbatem illius loci, regium assensum adhibuerimus et favorem, et velimus eidem electo ista vice gratiam facere in hac parte, vobis mandamus quod si contingat electionem illam per loci diœcesanum canonice confirmari, et vobis per litteras patentes ejusdem diœcesani inde constiterit evidenter, tunc, accepta nomine nostro ab eodem electo fidelitate nobis debita in hoc casu temporalia abbatiæ ejusdem sibi deliberari faciatis. Receptis tamen prius ab eodem electo litteris patentibus sigillo suo, necnon et sigillo capituli sui signatis, quod hæc gratia nostra non cedat in præjudicium seu trahatur in consequenciam temporibus futuris. In cujus, &c.

"Teste, ut supra" (*Hist. Doc. Rel. to Scot.*, Vol. II., pp. 106-7).

The brethren of the monastery met in their chapter on Friday, the Feast of St Matthew the Apostle, the same year, and sent certain of their fellow-canons to present Friar William of Jarum, the unanimously elected abbot, to the king, for the royal confirmation of the election, and they described him as "a man in every way fitted as abbot and pastor."

He witnessed a charter granted to Melrose Abbey. The same

abbot attended a meeting of Parliament at Ayr on 26th April 1315. The original ordinance is in the British Museum (*Harl. MS.*, 4694), and Sir James Balfour gives a list of the seals attached, one of them being that of the abbot of Jedburgh. That seal, however, along with others, had become broken, and has since entirely disappeared.

ROBERT. This abbot's name appears in the chartulary of Arbroath in 1322 and 1325, in the chartulary of Dryburgh in 1326, and in the chartulary of Kelso in 1329.

JOHN was abbot in 1338. He witnessed a grant to Dryburgh Abbey by William de Felton, the English Governor of Roxburgh Castle and Sheriff of Teviotdale. On 3rd April 1342 he witnessed a charter of David II., which was confirmed by Robert II. (Robertson's *Charters*). In 1343 he witnessed a confirmatory charter of King David Bruce to Kelso Abbey. In 1346 there was a treaty made at Roxburgh between Englishmen and the abbot of Jedburgh and other Scotsmen for settling the Scotch Borders (*Acta Parl.*, Vol. I., p. 180). He witnessed a charter of Edward III. to the church of St James at Roxburgh in 1354, and also one by Roger of Auldton to the chantry of St James, Roxburgh. It was probably this abbot who was present at Roxburgh in 1356 when Baliol made a formal concession of the kingdom of Scotland to Edward III.

ROBERT. This abbot went to England on the affairs of David II. in 1358, the year of that king's release from captivity, and was probably the abbot who was present at a meeting of Parliament held at Scone on 27th March 1371. The original instrument is in the General Register House, Edinburgh. The seals of those present, including that of the abbot of Jedburgh, were appended to the instrument, but unfortunately this abbot's seal is not now attached to the label or tag.

JOHN, who probably succeeded Abbot Robert, witnessed a charter of Robert III., confirming a charter of David II. in favour of Kelso Abbey, and dated at Scone 10th March 1390 (*Great Seal Register*, Vol. I.).

WALTER is the name of the next abbot of whom we find any notice. He, along with the abbots of Kelso, Melrose, and Dryburgh, was concerned in an agreement anent the corn tithes of Lessudden in 1444.

ANDREW, who was abbot in 1464, granted a right of burial in the choir in favour of Robert Rutherfurd of Chattow and his wife on 13th July that year.

ROBERT. In September 1473 Abbot Robert was, with several others, commissioned by James III. to meet with commissioners from the King of England, at Alnwick, for the redress of grievances and settling the conditions of truce. He attended the Parliaments held in Edinburgh in November 1469, May and August 1471, and March 1478. He still held the office in June 1478, as appears from the *Acta Dominorum Auditorum*, where reference is made to an action in which Sir William Steuart, knight, sued " Robert, abbot of Jedwert, anentis the wranguis withaldin fra him of the some of xv marcis of the malis of the lands of Stewartfeld, acht to the said William."

JOHN HALL was appointed by the king in December 1478, and attended the Parliament held in Edinburgh in October 1479. He assisted in restoring the abbey (see p. 43).

THOMAS CRANSTON was abbot in February 1484, and attended the Parliament held in Edinburgh in March that year. He also helped to restore the abbey (see pp. 45, 46).

ROBERT witnessed a charter by Walter Ker of Cessford on 20th October 1488, which, with the express consent of Robert, abbot of Kelso, and his convent, founded and constituted a perpetual chaplain to the altar of St Katherine the Virgin in the church of the monastery of Kelso on the north side of the same. James IV. confirmed this charter on 20th November the same year (*Great Seal Register*, Vol. II.).

THOMAS, abbot of Jedworth, was one of the Scottish commissioners at a meeting for a truce and redress of grievances held at

Coldstream on 25th March 1494 (*Cottonian MS., Caligula*, B. vii.). He is mentioned in the indenture of Canonby, dated 26th March of the same year (Armstrong's *Liddesdale*, App. No. X.).

ROBERT BLACKADER, archbishop of Glasgow, was commendator in 1504 (Pitcairn's *Criminal Trials*).

HENRY was appointed in April 1506 as one of the king's commissioners to let Kintyre, with all the isles south of the Point of Ardnamurchan, for money and grain rents, only for terms of three or five years. The commissioners had also extensive powers for the re-establishment of tranquillity in the Western Isles (*Exchequer Rolls*, Vols. XII. and XIII.). This abbot's name appears as witness to charters dated 1st December 1508, and 18th and 25th January 1512 (*Great Seal Register*, Vol. II.).

JOHN HOME, next abbot, was brother to the third Lord Home, Great Chamberlain of Scotland, who commanded the van of the Scottish army at the battle of Flodden. He was one of the witnesses to a confirming charter granted in Edinburgh on 16th August 1513 (*Great Seal*, Vol. II.). He sat in the Parliament held at Perth in November 1513, and in several held in Edinburgh afterwards. In 1516, when Lord Home and his brother William were treacherously put to death in Edinburgh, their brother, the abbot of Jedburgh, was banished beyond the Tay. He was elected Clerk of Expenses to the king in October 1526. In 1528, when Archibald Douglas, sixth Earl of Angus, was ordered by King James V. to be driven out of Scotland, the earl fortified himself in Tantallon Castle, from which he afterwards went to Coldingham Priory, of which his brother William had been prior. James, with 500 men, went thither to beard the lion in his den, and the king was accompanied by Lord Home and his brother, the abbot of Jedburgh, so that the latter might be placed in possession of the monastery. James placed Lord Home and his brother in possession, as was expected, but on the departure of the king Angus returned and expelled the intruders (*Douglas Book*, Vol. II., pp. 244, 245). In 1530 John Home sat as one of the Lords of Council (*Red Book of Monteith*). On 17th November 1537 this abbot granted a charter (confirmed by James V. on 26th January 1539-40) disposing in feu-farm to Andrew Gray and Janet Hume, his wife, the lands of Dunnynad, in the county of Forfar. This was done, as the charter bears, to meet the payment made by the abbot of the tax imposed by the Pope on the clergy and due to the king, and also for the rebuilding of the abbey, which had been burnt by the English (*Great Seal Register*, Vol. III.). In 1544 he was elected one of the Lords of the Articles. He, along with his brother, Lord Home, Lord Bothwell, and the abbot of Dryburgh, assisted by a number of Frenchmen, made an incursion into Northumberland on 15th August 1545. In the following year he protests for his teind penny of the composition of an escheat (*Acta Parl.*, Vol. II., 465A). On 26th March 1549 a charter of legitimation under the Great Seal was granted to Master John Home, Master Alexander Home, and Master Mathew Home, "bastardis filiis naturalibus reverendi in Christo patris Johannis de Jedburgh abbatis;" and on 20th April 1572 a similar charter was granted to John Home, "bastardo filio naturali quondam Johannis commendatarii de Jedburgh."

ANDREW HOME, nephew of the last abbot, and son of George, fourth Lord Home, was abbot commendator from 1560 till his death. He attended the Reformation Convention in 1560, and sat in the Parliament at Edinburgh in August 1567, and in several others held afterwards. He was present at a convention held in Holyrood House in March 1574, when delivery was made by Colin, Earl of Argyle, Dame Agnes Keith, his spouse, and others, of certain jewels which belonged to the king. In 1576 the Regent and Privy Council directed this abbot and others to meet at Canonby to take trial and inquisition, who were the "auld kindly tenants" and possessors of the same (Bruce Armstrong's *Liddesdale*, p. 117). The same year he was charged with intercommuning with traitors and rebels. This abbot must have died between 1593 and 1606. He was a commissioner for holding Parliament in 1593, and in the same year he was reponed to his right in the abbey, notwithstanding grants from the same; and in 1606 he is alluded to in an Act of Parliament as "umquhile Andrew, commendator of Jedburgh." He had for his seal, says Mr H. Laing, a representation of the Virgin and Infant Jesus standing within a Gothic niche. In the base of the seal is a shield, quarterly; first and fourth, a lion rampant for Home; second and third, three papingoes for Pepdie of Dunglas. Legend: S : ANDREE : COMMENDATARII : MONASTERII : DE : JEDBURGH (From a lead matrix in Dr Rawlinson's Collection, Bodleian Library, Oxford.) Another seal of this abbot bears a full-length figure of the Virgin and Child, standing within a Gothic niche. In the lower part of the seal is a shield quarterly with arms as above, and over all on a surtout an orle for Landels. Above the shield appears the head of a crosier. Legend as above. This is appended to a precept in favour of John, Lord Glammis, of the land of Little Cossins, 1561. Nisbet says he had seen a seal of this abbot having his arms cut, adorned only with a crosier (pastoral staff) erected in pale, placed at the back of the middle of the shield, the hooked head thereof appearing above the same turned inwards. Andrew's seal, as attached to the charter to William Scott of Haughhead, and to the precept of *clare constat* in favour of Mark Scott, already referred to, is simply a shield quarterly: the first and fourth a lion rampant, and the second and third three papingoes.

THE REFORMED CHURCH IN THE ABBEY.

ALTHOUGH several of the monasteries in Scotland suffered severely by the frantic enthusiasm of the populace in the Reformation against Popery—a few having been entirely demolished—it was the expressed desire of the leaders of the reforming party that the churches should be preserved. One good and sufficient reason for this was that they required them for the carrying on of their own worship. Not only would the throwing down of the churches have been a piece of wanton destruction, but the erection of new ones would have incurred a vast amount of unnecessary expense. The wrath of the Reformers, as has been truly remarked, was " against the warm, luxurious nests of monks and friars, and the deplorable cloisters of the miserable nuns, rather than against the fabrics appropriated only for divine worship." Jedburgh Abbey, as has been shown, suffered from other causes; and we may safely affirm that it sustained little or no injury at the time of the Reformation. The following order to the magistrates of burghs, issued on 12th August 1560, by the Lords of the Congregation, shows that, though it was recommended that the kirks should be freed from all monuments of idolatry, the kirks themselves were to be strictly preserved :—

"Our traist friendis, after maist hearty commendacion, we pray ze fail not to pass incontinent to the kirk, and tak down the haill images thereof, and bring furth to the kirkzyard, and burn thaym openly. And sicklyke cast down the alteris, and purge the kirk of all kynd of monuments of idolatrye. And this ze fail not to do, as ze will do us singular emplesur ; and so committis you to the protection of God. Fail not, bot ze tak guid heyd that neither the dasks, windocks, nor durris, be ony ways hurt or broken, either glassin work or iron work."

On 19th July 1560 Paul Methven, formerly of Dundee, was

nominated minister of Jedburgh by the Lords of the Congregation, and the church to which this minister came was under the tower of the abbey. It had probably been temporarily erected for the carrying on of worship by the canons after the destructive injuries sustained by the abbey in 1544-45.

On 13th September 1563 the Lords of the Privy Council, considering that kirks, partly by the sloth and negligence of parishioners, and partly by oversight of the parsons, are daily decaying and becoming ruinous, and part of them are already fallen down, the parishioners noways causing the same to be mended, nor yet the parson doing what appertains to him for upholding thereof, "quhairthrow the preching of the word of God, ministratioun of the sacraments, and reiding of the commone prayeris[1] ceissis and the people thairthrow becumis altogidder without knawlege and feir of God," ordained parish kirks that are decayed and fallen down be repaired and upbiggit, and where ruinous and faulty to be mended, two parts of the expense of future maintenance to be borne by the parishioners, and the third by the parson.

The first particular notice we have found of the state of the abbey church after the Reformation is in an Act of the Privy Council of date 9th February 1574-75, which shows that the Town Council and community of Jedburgh had raised letters setting forth that the roof and timber of the kirk were in so decayed a state as to call for immediate steps to prevent the falling down of the same. The complainers stated that, although it was the duty of the abbot to keep the kirk in proper repair, he had failed to do so, and they suggested that the timber of the refectory of the abbey should be taken down and used for that purpose. The Regent and Lords of Secret Council, after hearing Thomas Henderson on behalf of the burgh, and the abbot commendator for himself, complied with the request of the community, on condition that the commendator be asked to make no further repair on the kirk or "queir" at any

---

[1] Probably *The Book of Geneva*, drawn up by Knox and others in 1555. See Sprott and Leishman's Introduction to *The Book of Common Order*.

future time, unless the same were destroyed by the English, or by "sic vther accident maid ruinois." We give a copy of the Act of Council, as it is exceedingly interesting in many particulars :—

"Anent oure souerane lordis letters rasit at the instance of the prouest baillies counsall and comunitie of the burgh of Jedburgh makand mentioun That quhair thair paroche kirk quhilk aucht to be interteneit and vphaldin be the Abbot of Jedburgh persoun of the same is presentlie consumit and decayit in the rufe and tymmer thairof and within schort proces of tyme will all utirlie decay and fall doun gif tymous remeid be not prouidit thairto, And becaus the same is the saidis complenaris paroche kirk and becumis thame to se the reparatioun thairof for thair ressonabill ease at goddis seruice thairin, thay can find na better means to the help thairof than that the tymmer of the frater [or refectory] of the said Abbay, quhilk consumis and spillis and the place altogidder soliter, be tane doune and set vp and bestowit to the reparatioun and amendment of the ruif and tymmer werk of thair said paroche kirk, quhilk the abbot of the said abbay, albeit he sould interteny the same, he allwayis refuissis to do, expres aganis all ressoun and equitie, takand na regaird to the saidis complenaris quha myndis dalie god willing to assembill in the kirk to heir goddis word and call vpoun his holy name : And anent the charge gevin to the said Andro commendatare of Jedburgh to compeir befoir my lord Regentis grace and lordis of secreit counsall at ane certane day bipast, to heir and se gift and licence gevin to the saidis complenaris to tak doun and intromit with the tymmer of the said frater To the effect the same may be bestowit vpoun the reparatioun of the said paroche kirk for vphald thairof, or ellis to allege ane reassonabill caus quhy the samyn sould not be done, With certification to him and he failzeit my lord regentis grace and lordis foirsaidis wald decerne heirintill as accordis, Lyk as at mair lenth is contenit in the saidis lettres executioun and indorsatioun thairof : Quhilkis being callit, Thomas Hendersoun burges of the said burgh of Jedburgh comperand personallie in name and behalf of the inhabitantis of the said burgh and parochynnaris of the parochin of Jedburgh havand thair full power and commissioun, And the said commendatare being alsua personallie present, My Lord regentis grace with auise of the lordis of secreit counsale Ordanis, with consent of baith the saidis partiis, the tymmer of the said frater to be tane doun and to be apprysit be twa personis to be nominat and chosin be the saidis prouest baillies counsale and communitie of the said burgh, and vther twa personis to be nominat and chosin be the said commendatare, And that cautioun be fundin be the saidis prouest baillies counsale and communitie that the samyn tymmer, or the avale thairof as it sal be apprysit, with twa pairt alsmekill of expensis to be vpliftit of the inhabitantis of the said toun and paroche, sal be applyit to the reparatioun of the croce kirk within the said burgh for the ease and commoditie of the people resortand thairto at preching and prayer and na vtherwayis: Prouiding alwayis that the said commendatare be not chargeit to mak ony ferder expenssis vpoun the reparatioun of the said kirk or queir at this present or at ony tyme heireftir, Except the same be dimolissit and cassin doun be England, or be sic vther accident maid rwinois That thairthrow he be subject to repair the same for his pairt Conforme to the Act of parliament maid thairanent allanerlie."— Dated at Edinburgh, 9th February 1574-75 (*Privy Seal Register*).

It is impossible to ascertain the form or extent of the church which was thus repaired, and any conjecture as to these is attended with great difficulty. This church was never understood to have included any part of the choir of the abbey, and the idea that it might have included part of the nave seems discountenanced by the fact that in 1642, as will be seen by John Mill's report which is afterwards given, there was a great wall "under the steipill on the west syde."

By an Act of General Assembly in 1588 it was ordered that in future no burials should take place in the churches; but this seems not to have been enforced for some time, as we find that an overture for putting the Act into execution was, by the Assembly of 1638, referred to the care of presbyteries, and, on 29th July 1640, the presbytery of Jedburgh ordained that "in tymes coming ther sall be no corps buried in the kirks, and that conform to sundrie Acts of the Kirk."

Another order anent armorial bearings seems to have for some little time been disregarded, so that, on the 11th of August 1643, the Assembly, besides ratifying the Acts against burials in the kirks, inhibited and discharged all persons from hanging "pensils or boards," or affixing honours or arms, or making "any such like monuments, to the honour or remembrance of any deceased person, upon walls or other places within the kirk," where the public worship of God was exercised. In consequence of this, Mr William Jamieson, minister of Jedburgh, on 24th January 1644, "regrates to the presbytrie the affixing of honours and arms within the kirk of Jedburgh that is suffered to remane," notwithstanding the Act of Assembly against the same. The presbytery "ordeanes the samine to be takin doune, and referrs it to the minister and session to acquaint my lord Ballmirrino or any other having interess therewith and *primo quoque tempore* to report ther dilligence heerin."

In 1636 one of the "pryme pillars" which supported the tower was reported to be in a dangerous state, but no immediate steps seem to have been taken to improve its condition. In February 1642 the presbytery met for visitation of the kirk. On that occasion the minister, William Jamieson, "being demandit what he had to say against his parochiners," thanked God that many of his parishioners loved the word, and "wer reverend hearers thairof and frequented God's house. 3 things wer regraitted by him. First, that discipline had neid to be helpit in respect of former negligence of the vse thairof quhairthrow many vyces had aboundit; Secondlie, that his people durst not conveene without danger; Thirdly, that the kirk is too little for containing the whole Parochin." The heritors agreed to approve of whatever was ordered by the presbytery, and John Mill, a "maister of work," having been brought from Edinburgh for the purpose of getting his "advyce to sie with masons quhat wer the dangers of the house, and quhat way it micht be repairit," reported that "the mending of the piller will cost a thousand merks, and thrie scoir singill tries, threttie double tries, two hundreth daills to be scaffolding and centtries." Mr Mill's report proceeds as follows :—

"For enlarging of the kirk 4 arches—three pillers—the building up of the west gawell so high as convenientlie may serve the height of the syde walls of the said kirk, with ane window to the west on the said gawell, and ane fair doore for entrie in good and sufficient stone work. Secondlie, so far of the said kirk as is to be advancit, the height of the walls thairof takin down to the crown of the great arches and the walls of that place levellit for the roofe. Lykwyse the syd flankers of the said kirk wpon the south and north syde takin down so far that ane roofe to-fa wayis may theik vnder the eising of the body of the kirk, and lykwayis the same to be levellit at that place, and the windows thairof sloppit doune and archit again so far as convenientlie they might serve the kirk with light. Thirdlie, the great wall that standeth vnder the steipill on the west syde to be taken doun, ane fair arch to be betwixt the 2 pillars on the south and north thairof and then built wp of solid stone work to the greit heich arch of the steippill, for the quhilk doeing and repairing the sowme of ane 1000 libs. Item for 700 daillis, 700 merks; Item for making of the roofe and sarking of it, and setting of it up, 300 mks.; Item for sklaittis and sklaitting, 500 mks.; Item for naills, 200 mks.; Item for glasse, 300 mks.; Item for iron work, 100 libs.; Item for Lyme, 500 libs. The maister of work reports he thinks it is a wonder how either the minister dar be bold to preach or the people to heir" (*Presbytery Records*).

In his examination of the kirk Mill was assisted by Robert Mein, mason, Newstead; Thomas Ker, mason, Jedburgh; George Busbie, wright, Kelso; William Robson and Andrew Robson, wrights, Kelso; and John Williamson, glazier-wright; and they all declared the great "necessitie of helping and repairing the kirk, and for preventing the ruin and fall thairof," and that it was dangerous for the people to meet there "without speidie and tymous help for provyding remedie." The presbytery having approved of the same, exhorted the parishioners most earnestly to meet, and cause a stent roll to be made up for the purpose of raising the necessary funds, and advised them to use all possible diligence to have the work speedily carried out; and on the 27th July 1643 they recommended to the care of the General Assembly "anent quhat way sall be thought fit for collecting of a supply for repairing of the kirk of Jedburgh."

On 15th July 1646 the presbytery approved of the act of session of Jedburgh about the communion tables standing as they stood at the communion till "a way be found for enlarging the kirk."

The alterations and additions proposed by Mill would have cost

£383, 6s. 8d. sterling, and when we take into account that money then was at least six times more value than at present—which would be equal to £2300 at this time—it will be seen that the expense was considerable, and ought to have improved the kirk very materially. It is certain, however, notwithstanding the apparent anxiety of those interested to have the work done, that Mill's plan was never carried out. There can be no doubt that some repairs were effected shortly after Mill's report, and towards the payment of these 1300 merks were borrowed from John Ker of West Nisbet. On 14th May 1653 the Town Council assessed for the burgh's share of the sum borrowed, and it was resolved that "troopers be quartered upon those who refuse to pay the stent in the burgh." The town officers, it appears, collected the "kirk money," and in June the council resolved to imprison "deficients of the stent roll for kirk timber."

It is evident that no allocation of the church had taken place previous to 1640, and that the "localities" were about this time assigned by the minister and session, subject to appeal to the presbytery, as appears from the fact that in that year the Laird of Edgerston (yr.) supplicated the brethren of the presbytery "for a place in the kirk of Jedburgh quhair he is a parochiner. The brether gif warrant to him to keip the place quhair he vsed to sitt vntill a minister be settled in Jedburgh." The presbytery having remitted the arrangement of this same matter afterwards to Thomas Abernethy, minister of Hownam, the Laird of Edgerston complained that Mr Abernethy had infringed the acts formerly made by the minister and session anent the seat, and that he had gone beyond his commission, and had meddled with things that did not accord therewith. The presbytery declared what he had done to be null and void, and the acts made by the session and minister of Jedburgh "before his going to the army" to be of the same vigour, force, and strength as before. In the same year the Laird of Hunthill gave into the presbytery "ane bill compleaning he was wronged in his seat in the kirk, and desyring he micht not be wronged." This is referred to Mr Jamieson, the minister, "who is now at the armie." The question having not been so speedily or so satisfactorily settled as the complainer would have wished, he seems to have taken the somewhat bold step of bringing it to an end by a lock-out, as may be inferred from the presbytery records of date 29th October 1642, where it is stated that the Laird of Hunthill delivered the key of the door between the kirk and the " queir," that free entry might be made to the people to convene in the service of God.

The Town Council having resolved to build a council house, they appointed a committee in March 1664 to speak with certain parties anent the "redding of the ground, and houking out of some stains at fraters' gawell," and to agree with them for the same. The treasurer was afterwards authorised to pay the workmen a groat a day for their meat. On the 4th of the following month the council appointed the magistrates to speak with the heritors anent the downtaking of any ruinous part about the kirk, and "especially the rinks, which are most dangerous, and to desire the stones thereof to help to build the council house."

In 1666 the kirk was again in need of repair, and the minister, Peter Blair (who had been presented by Charles II., and had conformed to Episcopacy), advised the magistrates not to "refuis to send for mesones to sight the kirk, if the heritors put it upon them, quilk being voyced about, the Counsell condischendit before the work be retardit that they sould condischend thairto." John Fall, mason, appears to have been ordered to inspect the kirk, and extensive alterations seem to have been resolved upon. The Town Council resolved voluntarily to give 2500 merks as their share, and appointed a commission to proceed to Glasgow to ask the archbishop and synod for a contribution towards the work. They applied also to the synod of Dumfries for a contribution. On 14th September 1667 the council appointed William Young to go with the minister to Glasgow to bring home the money which had been contributed for the kirk; but the minister informed the provost that the contribution could not be had until caution was found that it be employed for repairing of "the whole fabric," and the provost gave caution to that effect. The presbytery contributed "333 lbs." towards the work. On 16th November the council "ordains James Fall to be satisfied of the sum of £200 for timber bought by him from my Lord Newbattle for the rebuilding of the kirk. Ordains George Rutherfurd, treasurer, to satisfy David Schairif and Ralph Robson, in Oxnam, the leaders of the wood for the use of the kirk, the sum of £19 Scots money." In January 1668 it was resolved by the council to write to the archbishop of Glasgow to desire a visitation of the kirk. William Haswell, late bailie, was appointed to go with the letter, and the magistrates and Dr Simson and James Cubie were to give the ex-bailie his instructions. He afterwards reported that his "voyadge" to the archbishop had cost "38 lbs." Thus far the work of repairing the kirk under the tower seemed likely to be accomplished on a somewhat extensive plan—may it not have been that recommended by Mill twenty-six years before?—but still it never was effected. The burgh records of date 28th May 1668 bear that "the provost signified that he had met with my Lord Ker and Sir Thomas Ker, and that my lord desired the burgh would consent to give for *rebuilding the old fabric or rinks*[1] for their proportion 2500 merks, by and altour the 1000 merks for the contribution, and to bring home the third part of the lime and timber." This was something altogether different from what had been previously proposed; it was, in short, a suggestion to leave the church under the tower, and to build one in the nave. The provost and Andrew Ainslie were authorised by the town and heritors to meet with his lordship and Sir Thomas anent the repairing or rebuilding of "ane capacious church." The council all in one voice consented to the proposal of his lordship, and during the following month the provost reported that an agreement had been made with James Fall anent the kirk. On the 18th of July "the council condescends that there be a voluntary contribution for the building of the kirk, and to that effect the minister, with an elder and the bailie of his quarter, to go through the town *domatim* upon Wednesday next. The

---

[1] Popularly called "links." The derivation of the word as here applied is very obscure.

council condescends for furnishing forty bags of lime; that the council being twenty-four in number, they, with sixteen to be added, shall furnish, either of them, one bag of lime, and that there be no less than four fulls in every bag, at least what the heritors bring, and that they bring in the same within four days after advertisement, under pain of half-a-crown every bag." The sixteen persons added to the council for this good work were Daniel Porteous, Adam Wilson, Janet Champnay, Andrew Jerdon, Issobel Robson, John Wilson, John Yong, Richard Dick, Stephen Robson, William Brown, Thomas Porteous, Alexander Cunningham, Christian Rutherfurd, James Robson, William Brown, and William Rutherfurd of the Hall. The council seem to have been afraid that the new church might even prove too small, for we find that on 12th September, just three months after they had arranged as to the bringing in of the lime for the building, they "all in ane voice condescend to take in another pillar to the church for enlarging thereof." The new church at the west end of the nave appears to have been completed and allocated or "divided" in 1671. The Ten Commandments and Creed were painted on the plaster on the east gable, where, no doubt, the altar was, and above each of the large pillars was painted a text of Scripture. Portions of these were seen up to the time when the church was removed from the abbey. This new and capacious church extended to the fifth pillar from the west end, and included north and south aisles. Besides the principal entrance at the west end, there were two doorways on the north side, and one on the south by which the minister entered. In 1691 Lady Mangerton built a loft in a place claimed by Edgerston.

In 1692 Robert, Lord Jedburgh, presented a new bell to the kirk.

On 31st October 1702 the Town Council discharged all inhabitants, masons, or others within the burgh from meddling with, or any way making use of any of the kirk stones, under pain of £10, "and other punishment besides."

On 14th November of the same year the council recommended that a committee represent to the kirk-session that there should be "ane collection for the casting of the little kirk bell." On 3rd April 1703 the council appointed a committee to speak with the session, and to show them that the council " desires that intimation be made from the pulpit for a collection at the kirk door for payment of the little kirk bell's casting, stocking, and other expenses relating thereto, and also to overture the session that what it may extend to in all may be borrowed by the burgh and session, in regard the same is lying ready at Edinburgh." A committee was appointed by the council on 2nd March 1706 to inspect the bells, and "sie they be sound in their hanging upon the stocks." In 1726-27 the church was repaired, and at this time the pillars were cut for the purpose of laying joists. In 1727 Provosts Richardson and Douglas obtained "liberty to build lofts" over the localities of the Marquess of Lothian, Sir J. Rutherfurd, and Bonjedward, on condition that they surrender them when required on payment of cost of erection.

A committee of the Town Council met on 10th January 1729 anent the kirk bells, and Bailie Martin, in name of the kirk-session, produced an extract from the records of the session, wherein it was set forth that the session had in the year 1694 expended the sum of £333, 6s. 4d. Scots out of the poors' money in maintaining and hanging the great bell mortified to the kirk by the late Lord Jedburgh, and the Town Council had by an act appropriated the bells to their own use, and had for about thirteen years past uplifted the emoluments of the said bell "gotten at the funerals of the dead," notwithstanding that they had been at no expense regarding it. The session therefore required a reimbursement of the said sum expended, and a renunciation of any pretensions the town might have to the emoluments of the said bell, and that for the future the emoluments might belong to the poor. The committee, after considering the matter, were of opinion that the town was not obliged to pay the sum "wared out" in a work which concerned the whole parish; and as the ringing of the bells in all royal burghs was at the direction of the magistrates, they thought this point ought not to be given up without further consideration.

There was an allocation of the church this same year in consequence of the repairs on the fabric, and this was made on the basis of the original division by Douglas of Timpendean, Stewart of Stewartfield, and the magistrates, appointed by the heritors for that purpose (*Heritors' Records*). On 18th April a meeting of the deacons of the trades and the convener, Andrew Robson, was held in order for "settling, nominating, and appointing the new loft," at which it was resolved that the first seat be possessed by the quartermasters and boxmasters in office for the time, the second seat by the freemen, and the third and fourth by the journeymen and apprentices; and for the better keeping of the same seats the officers of the trades were appointed to attend each Sabbath day, to see that the sitters in the seats bred no disturbance, under the penalty of being punished conform to law (*Minute Book of the Fleshers' Trade*). Difficulties in regard to sittings seem to have been somewhat frequent. In October 1732 the magistrates were appointed by the heritors to settle the Lanton localities, and on the original division having been read over, it was found that the Marquess of Douglas and his tenants were to sit betwixt the pillar on the west side of the pulpit, according to his valuation, and the rest of that place for Lanton and the tenants there, "ilk ane of them having several breasts," as also that the heritors of Lanton were further to have the part under Lord Rutherfurd's loft for their locality, excepting two pews in the fore part for his lordship. Madder's lands, having been found to extend to about half the whole valuation of Lanton, had assigned to them two pews immediately behind Sir John Rutherfurd's seat, each seat extending in length from pillar to pillar, and breadth two feet two inches, a free entry to be through this ocality to Sir John Rutherfurd's seat. The ground immediately behind Madder's back seat was given to Alexander Ferguson, "to the end that he might erect a half seat there." The Duke of Buccleuch was to have a seat extending from the wall on the east side of the meikle kirk door to the entry that led into Cavers Carr's seat, keeping always within the general locality of Lanton.

In 1735 the magistrates were appointed to "take inspection"

JEDBURGH ABBEY from the NORTH-EAST in 1775.

what might be necessary to prevent the church being abused by swallows. How different is this sentiment from that expressed by the Psalmist—" Yea, the sparrow hath found an house, and the swallow a nest for herself, where she may lay her young, even thine altars."

In the early part of February 1743 the crown arch of the abbey tower fell, as appears from the Town Council Records. A special meeting of the magistrates and council, with several of the principal inhabitants, was held on 31st January 1743, to hear and consider a report of Thomas Winter, mason, anent the condition of the "steeple-head and pend." Winter reported that at the desire of the magistrates he had that day visited the "steeple-head and pend," and found the same in a "ratcht" and dangerous condition, and that to all appearance it would fall down. He therefore recommended that the bells and clock should be taken down as soon as possible, in order to prevent their being destroyed, because if the rent should become wider it would be dangerous for workmen to go up and take them down; and he further recommended that if it was intended to repair the steeple-head and hang up the bells there, the pend should be struck down, and the bartizan and head of the wall should be taken down to the onset of the pend, and a roof raised. The meeting resolved to have the bells removed, and to acquaint the heritors of what had occurred. On the 14th of February the magistrates and council again met, when Bailie Jerdon informed them that since their last meeting the "pend" had fallen down, and that it was the opinion of tradesmen that nothing could be done as to the taking down of the bells without having "great timber from Berwick," which could not be got at that season of the year. A committee was appointed to lay before the heritors the ruinous and dangerous state of the steeple, " especially the south-east part thereof, which lies next to the Grammar School," whereby the said school was in the greatest danger.[1] Reference to the falling of the tower

---

[1] It is generally believed that the little chapel south of the choir had been for some time used as the Grammar School, but a number of entries in local records in reference to the repairing, &c., of the school previous to this date are such as

arch is made also in a memorial by the Magistrates and Town Council of date 1758 to the Convention of Royal Burghs on the decayed state of the town, and praying for ease and relief of their stent. The memorial sets forth, *inter alia*, that about three years ago their county jail was declared ruinous and unfit for the purposes of a jail, which obliged them to take down and rebuild the same, and as the arch of their great steeple was fallen down, whereby the bells and clock, which were very valuable, were in great danger, the then magistrates and council very wisely thought proper in rebuilding their jail to carry up four pillars in the midst thereof, in order to hang the bells and put up the said clock therein. The building here referred to developed subsequently into the present town steeple, in which the bells are now hung.

In 1744 the back door of the church leading into the minister's garden was repaired, and the "arch above the scholars' loft" in the kirk was ordered to be struck down. Six years after this the pulpit was ordered to be fixed.

The Laird of Bonjedward took down some vaults near to Abbotshall in 1748, as appears from the records of a case in the Sheriff Court, to which reference is made afterwards.

The church was again in need of repair in 1759, and in connection with this the heritors authorised the digging up of and the taking of stones from below the tower.

---

to render this more than doubtful. The school is spoken of as having chimneys and being thatched with broom, conditions that could not possibly apply to this chapel. It is certain, however, that at this time the school was in close proximity to the chapel, either inside or immediately outside of the abbey, and that it was removed in 1751 to premises in Canongate, rented by the magistrates for that purpose. It was to this school in Canongate that the father of Sir David Brewster came as rector in 1771, and there he taught for several years, until another school was erected at the top of the Dean's Close. It is recorded in the Jedburgh Town Council Records that, in July 1756, the magistrates applied to the heritors for liberty to take the "stones in the old Latin School"—that is, the Grammar School at the abbey—for use in the erection of the town steeple. In 1764 the heritors ordered the schoolhouse door and gable to be built up.

PLAN OF THE ABBEY KIRK OF JEDBURGH WITH THE MANSE,

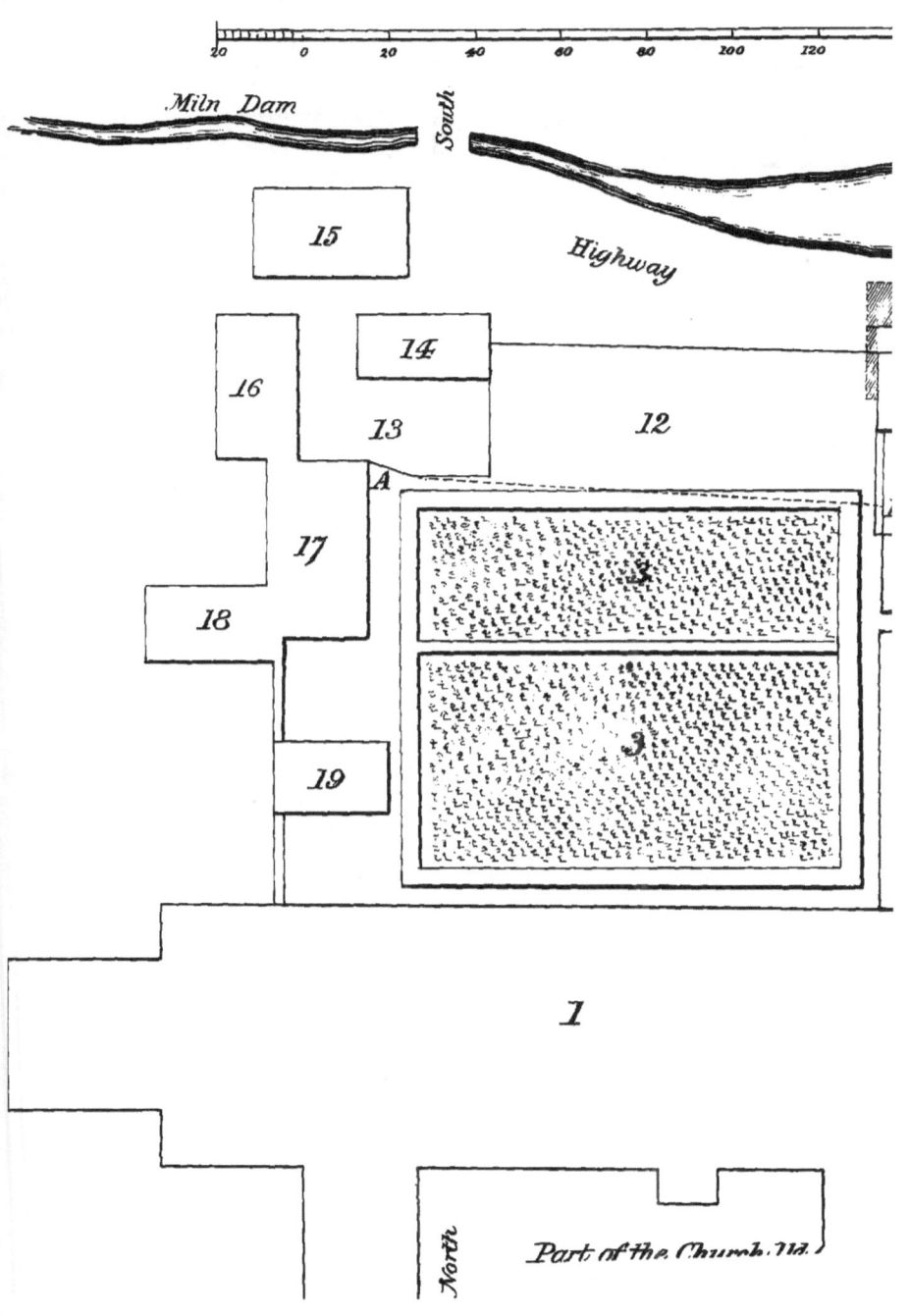

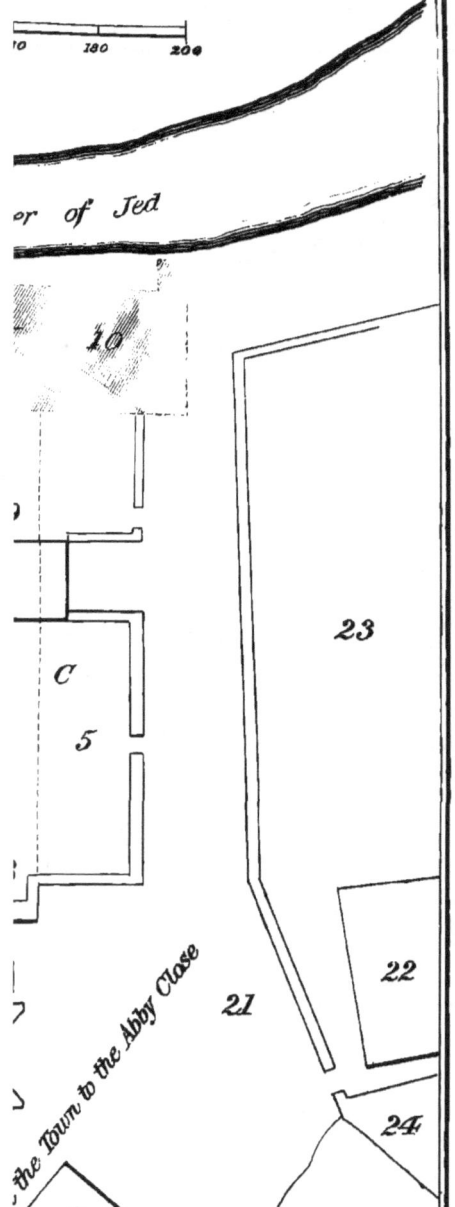

REFERENCES.

No 1—The Kirk
 2—The Manse
 3—The Garden
 4—Brew-house and stable
 5—The Court in dispute
 6—The Coal House
 7—The Cellar
 8—The Necessary House
 9—Minister's Barn Yard
 10—The Foundation of Abbot's Hall
 11—Minister's Barn
 12—The Bank in dispute
     (*Strawberry Bank*)
 13—Mitchell's Yard 10 feet perpendicular lower than the Minister's Yard
 14—Mitchell's Stable
 15—The Town House
 16—Mitchell's House
 17—Andrew Preston's House
 18—John Preston's House
 19—Vault in the Garden
 20—Part of a range of houses upon the north side of Abbey Close
 21—Abbey Close
 22—The Wren's Nest
 23—The Wren's Nest Yard
 24—Part of Waugh's Yard

Jedburgh, February 19 1760.

James Winter,

N.B. Nos 13 14 and 16 were the Town's Property and sold to the Mitchells.

From the evidence in a case before the Court of Session in 1760, relative to certain alleged encroachments made by the minister and heritors of Jedburgh on the town's property, we glean some interesting particulars, which show that shortly before that time many fragments of the abbey buildings existed, of which there are now no traces; and the better to enable the reader to understand them, we give a copy of a plan prepared for the court at the time (see plan). We may mention in this connection that in 1669 the magistrates purchased from the Lothian family Bongate, Richmond, Abbey Close, and the high and laigh kirkyards—all abbey property—and that the charter granted to the burgh in 1671 by Charles II. excepts, among other subjects, the Abbey Kirk, the cloisters on the south side of the kirk, the Old Hall, Wren's Nest, Dabie's Tower, and a tower near the Cross, at the south-west corner of Market Place. The magistrates alleged that there had been taken in from Abbey Close all outside the pricked line at No. 5 of plan, and that portion from 10 to 9; and that the strawberry bank (No. 12) formed no part of the cloisters, as contended by the other parties. The case was decided in favour of the minister and heritors. We may also mention that of all the houses marked on the plan the only one remaining is the Wren's Nest, and that the old mill wear or cauld shown on the plan is also a thing of the past.

Among the documents produced in the above case was a disposition by Thomas Rutherfurd of that Ilk, dated 15th June 1714, in favour of the Magistrates and Town Council of "all and haill these old vaulted walls and schoolhouse, &c., lying within the abbacy and the burgh, in the laigh kirkyard thereof, bounded between the convent kirkyard on the east, the house pertaining to the Abbey Mill and mill dam on the south, the minister's yard on the west, and the tenement pertaining to the heirs of John Wood, wheelwright, on the north parts."

James Winter, formerly a bailie in the burgh, who made the plan produced, remembered the minister's corn-stacks being set on the pend or arch on the east side of the easter gable of Abbotshall. The eastern gable was tushed in the corners, as if more buildings had been joined to it, or intended to be joined to it, on the north corner. The south corner was tushed in the same way, and there were the remains of a turnpike stair at the south corner, on the east side of the gable. The pricked line at No. 10 shows the site of Abbotshall.[1] Other witnesses remembered seeing boys climb up the bindwood on the eastern gable to the top of it, and also seeing them jump from a window on the north side. From the evidence of other witnesses we learn that the magistrates bought from John Preston a vault that stood on the south-west corner of his house (No. 18), and that the stones were carried away to repair the wauk mill. The vault extended about twelve feet west into the garden, and it was about eight feet the other way. There was a house between that which belonged to Turner, near the west end of No. 13, and the miller's house on the dam-side (No. 15), and there was a vault from the west end of that house with a large arch on the south gable, and this vault was like the building of the old abbey. After Turner's death it was sold to Rutherford of Hunthill, and Rutherford sold it to the magistrates, who applied the stones to the building of the flesh market. Most of Turner's house was built of ashlar. Two pillars stood near the west of Mitchell's stable (No. 14), rather within the south dyke of No. 12, which pillars and the spaces between them were covered with hewn stones. Mr Winchester, the minister (1734-55), took up some vaults on the north side of the strawberry bank, under the then south wall of the garden; and there were pieces of old work at a distance from one another on the south and west sides. The old manse, occupied by Mr Semple (1690-1706), was spoken of as consisting of a long house called "the gallery," part of which stood north and south, and a jamb that went east and west from the south end of the gallery part. The wester gable of the jamb, which was partly old work built of ashlar, was at the western gable of the brew-house and stable (No. 4).

---

[1] A portion of the outer wall of the abbey is still seen at the mill lade at the foot of Abbey Close, and there are two openings at the base which must have communicated with Abbotshall, probably for sanitary purposes. At that time the base of the wall was washed by the river.

At the west corner of the kirk was a vault, which the minister converted into a cow-byre. One witness spoke of little pends or holes which led to a passage underground that ran from west to east near the south walk of the garden. The minister's corn was brought from the glebe on the south side of the Jed in sleds over the western dam bridge, and from thence up to the Bow at Abbotshall, and there forked up to the stackyard, there being no sledge-way along the south side of the rumbling dyke at the foot of the strawberry bank. We have heard from time to time of workmen coming upon subterranean passages in the course of their work, but these have always been filled up before investigation was made.

Some time after the above action was finished the Laird of Abbotrule began to search for vaults at the site of Abbotshall, with the intention, as he said, of selling the stones for building purposes, and he alleged that the minister's barn (No. 11 of plan) had been erected on his (Abbotrule's) property. Mr Douglas, the minister (1758-68), denied Abbotrule's right to the property, and held that the charter which gave him "all and haill of the great hall within the precincts of the town of Jedburgh, called the Old Hall, with vaults, houses, biggings," &c., could give him no claim to Abbotshall, which was within the abbacy, and barony of Ulston, and paid no stent; as well might he commence to search in the manse garden, where it was believed that in many places would be found great numbers of vaulted cloisters and cells. Besides, the vaults at Abbotshall had been removed in 1748 by the Laird of Bonjedward, to whom they had been sold. Regardless of all remonstrance, Abbotrule set several men to work on the disputed ground, which resulted in the bringing down of the barn while the minister was in church engaged in preparatory services for the sacrament on the following day. This case was also settled in court in favour of the minister.

Mr Douglas had good cause to suspect that he had been subjected to this annoyance on the part of the magistrates in revenge for his having been presented to the parish instead of the man of their choice, Mr Thomas Boston, minister of Oxnam; and Abbotrule, "who had been a protector of the complainer against the ill-treatment of the magistrates, now joined them in affronting and distressing him," he (Abbotrule) being a young man and ill advised. Mr Douglas stated that, for his own part, if Abbotrule was led to take these steps by the advice of others, as an insult upon the complainer, and to throw contempt upon him in the eyes of the parishioners, he freely and heartily forgave him, and humbly hoped that, by the assistance of Divine Providence, the many unjust rubs which had been thrown upon him, and the persecution which he had suffered, would one day entitle him to find favour in the eyes of every well-disposed person among the people over whom he had been placed as pastor, and whose spiritual improvement and instruction would ever be the chief wish of his heart and labour of his life. The alleged encroachments were made by the predecessor of Mr Douglas some twelve years previously, apparently without opposition, but this was said to have been due to "the negligence of former managers."

The heritors, considering that the kirk steeple and abbey were greatly damaged by boys and others climbing upon the walls, a resolution was passed in June 1761 prohibiting the same in future, parents and masters to be responsible for their children and servants; but it seems that this prohibition had not the desired effect, for three years afterwards an order was given for the building up of the old school-house door and gable, "and every place boys get up to the steeple."

In 1764 it was reported to the heritors that the bells, clock, and weather-cock were in hazard, in consequence of the ruinous state of the belfry, which was all rent and dangerous. After various visitations to the belfry by tradesmen from Kelso, Newstead, and Jedburgh, it was reported in June 1771 that "the bells must be removed, and the sooner the better." Bailie Winter estimated the cost of taking down the bells from the abbey tower and putting them up in the new steeple at £20 sterling, the workmen not to be responsible for any damage which might be sustained by the bells. The heritors seem not to have been prepared to give this sum, but they agreed to have the bells removed as soon as tradesmen could

JEDBURGH ABBEY *from the* NORTH *in* 1777

be got to do the work for £10, and to be responsible for any damage through insufficiency of material or workmanship. In August of the same year a contract was entered into with James Ovens and Robert Balmer, who undertook the work for the latter sum, and it was agreed that they should have the use of the "town's machinery." After the removal of the bells, the clock, which still remained in the belfry, became silent, and the managers of the town (there were no magistrates at this time), after taking this into consideration, resolved that a board be put up so that the clock might be heard. They also applied for estimates for taking down the clock, repairing it, and putting it up in the new steeple. The old clock was never, however, put into the new steeple, as a new clock with four dials and pointers was afterwards ordered to be made. The removal of the belfry from the abbey tower is afterwards referred to.

One of the bells removed from the abbey—"the little kirk bell" referred to on page 91—was sent to the Royal Mines Company, London, in exchange for a new one. The bells now hanging in the town steeple are three in number, viz.—(1) that presented to the kirk by Robert, Lord Jedburgh, in 1692: (2) that popularly called the court bell (the one supplied by the Royal Mines Company); and (3) the alarm bell.

While collecting materials for the first edition of this work in 1877 we had occasion to visit the town steeple for the purpose of examining Lord Jedburgh's bell. At the same time we made an examination of the alarm bell, and were agreeably surprised to find, what had not been suspected before, that it bore the following inscription in beautiful old characters, "+ CAMPANA : BEATE : MARGARETE : VIRGINIS"—the bell of the Blessed Margaret the Virgin. The bell is 18 inches in diameter at the mouth and 14 inches high. The Rev. H. T. Ellacombe, The Rectory, Clyst St George, Topsham, an authority on the subject of old bells, had his attention called to this interesting discovery by a communication in *Notes and Queries*, and having had a rubbing of the inscription submitted to him, he gave it as his opinion that this was a sanctus bell, and probably belonged to the abbey. "The words," he says, "were intended for a leonine verse, but the founder has made a blunder, and placed two words out of order. Founders often made such blunders, frequently putting letters upside down. The correct line would be thus: 'CAMPANA : MARGARETE : VIRGINIS : BEATE,' or made so that 'Beate' and 'Margarete' should run in rhyme. The date of the bell is the fifteenth century." It is right to say that other authorities have fixed the fourteenth century as the probable date.

On 15th April 1779 "the bartizan" of the steeple, above Rutherfurd's aisle, was ordered to be taken down, being in a dangerous state, and the stones were to be applied to the building of the Latin School.

In 1789 William Thorburn, mason, reported that eleven of the pillars above "the leads"—*i.e.*, the pillars of the clerestory above the roof of the church—were wasted and dangerous, and that two "butts," one on each side of the great door, were in the same state. He suggested that where the small pillars were decayed they "might be supplied with posts of oak, being less expensive than stone;" and the heritors resolved to put wooden pillars behind the stone pillars which were wasted.

In January 1792, in consequence of a report on the unsatisfactory condition of the church, and considering the great expense required to put it into a proper state, the heritors thought it would be well to build a new church, and appointed a committee to look out for a site, and to procure estimates for the building of a church to hold 1500 persons. The report on the state of the church at this time is interesting, as it shows that at this late period the groined roofed side aisles still existed. The words of the report are: "All *arches between the pillars and outside walls within the church* seem unsafe, and ought to be taken down, and as *these arches support the slated roof on the north side*, that roof ought to be taken down," &c. The estimate for the suggested repairs was £504, 12s. 7d., which included £3 for whitewashing and painting the pillars. This plan, as we have already stated, did not meet with the approval of the heritors; but the idea of a new church was also departed from. Several other plans were considered, and ultimately one by Mr

William Elliot, Cavers, was approved of, the estimated cost of carrying out of which was £774, 16s. 7d. Contracts were entered into with Mr Elliot, Mr Winterup, and Mr Balmer for executing the repairs, and the work was to be finished on or before 10th April 1793. It was at this time that the south aisle was removed, and the wall brought forward to the pillars, so as to make the lightest and most comfortable church with least expense. The lower windows on the south side were to be raised to the top of the arches, and windows were also inserted in the arches of the triforium. The north aisle was to be taken down and rebuilt, and instead of two doorways in that wall as formerly, there was to be but one, with two windows on each side 3 feet wide by 5 feet high. In the area of the church there were to be several square seats $5\frac{1}{2}$ feet wide, extending to the front of the north pillars, and it was arranged that four of the seats in the middle of the church were to be movable, in order that at the time of the sacrament a double row of tables might be set, one along these seats, and one along the area opposite, with a passage for the elders along one side of each. New galleries were also put in at this time.

It having been reported to the heritors in May 1804 that there was great danger in part of the overhanging wall of the abbey, they resolved to take down the dangerous parts, probably portions of the vaulted roof of the aisles. In the following year they passed a resolution to prevent all persons from taking stones from the old building.

In 1818 the top of the west gable was reported to be dangerous, in consequence of water having got in at the skew, and it was resolved to remove part of the masonry and to cover the top with lead, till the proper repairs could be executed. Mr James Gillespie, Edinburgh (who built the county prison about this time on the site of the old castle), submitted a plan in 1822 for the rebuilding of the upper part of the gable, so as to "stand as long as any portion of the abbey." This was approved of, the same to cost about £50 or £60, most of which was for scaffolding. About the same time material repairs were carried out on the great tower; an iron belt was put round the walls, which were further protected by the putting in of two strong iron rods. This part of the work was according to plans by Mr Archibald Elliot, architect, London. The heritors and magistrates, together with the owners of property within the county, applied to the Barons of Exchequer for an allowance from the fund at their disposal for such purposes towards the payment of the repairs, but the application was not entertained. The expense was partly, if not solely, defrayed by public subscription.

The end walls of Rutherfurd's aisle, which had been taken down to give a better view of the abbey, were, in May 1827, ordered to be rebuilt, to prevent trespassers from getting in. In 1831 the question of building a new church or repairing the old one was again revived, and again it was held that a new church was inexpedient. Repairs and alterations costing £280 were ordered, but these were found insufficient, and further alterations were found to be necessary. In 1867 great inconvenience was experienced in consequence of there not being a proper allocation of the seatings, and as it was believed that a re-allocation was impossible under the then existing circumstances, it was thought that the erection of a new church was the only way to remedy the grievance.

The late Marquess of Lothian, who from his earliest years evinced a remarkable love for the abbey of Jedburgh, and very justly held it to be one of the finest of all the abbeys of Scotland, long cherished the hope of seeing the beautiful ruins cleared of all modern patchwork. With this view his lordship entered into negotiations with the heritors of the parish, and offered to contribute largely towards the erection of a new church on condition that the old church should be removed from the abbey. There was only one opinion regarding the state of the old church, and it was that a very considerable sum would be required before it could be made a comfortable place of worship. Instead of accepting his lordship's liberal offer, however, the heritors resolved to carry out a plan by Mr George Bell, architect, Glasgow, for the improvement of the old church. This plan, the carrying out of which was estimated to cost between £4000 and £5000, provided for the clearing away of the rubble walling between the pillars and arches in the first and second storeys on the south side, and for the restoring of the south aisle. This was to allow the galleries, upper and lower, to be removed, and the north wall was to be reduced in height so as to open to view the second tier of arches on that side. The principal roof was to be raised to its original position, so as to restore to the church the clerestory, the west window, and the St Catherine's wheel. To open up to view the whole length of the interior, it was suggested by Mr Bell to substitute a glass screen for the dead wall which served as the eastern gable; and it was proposed to insert glass in the arches of the triforium, as well as in the windows of the clerestory. The carrying out of this plan, however, involved the taking in part of the old building which did not belong to the heritors, and they were consequently interdicted by the marquess. Matters being thus brought to a deadlock, Lord Lothian, finding that no response was made to his previous liberal offer, proposed to bear the whole expense of a new church, and this was ultimately accepted by the heritors. But it was not the lot of his lordship to see any part of the work accomplished, as he died before the negotiations were completed. The present marquess, with praiseworthy zeal, determined to carry out the wishes of his late lamented brother, and they were fulfilled in a highly generous spirit. The closing services in the abbey church took place on the 4th of April 1875, and the new parish church, a very handsome structure in the Early English style of architecture (Mr T. S. Wyatt, London, architect), was opened for worship on the following Sunday.

Jedburgh Abbey thus ceased to be a place of worship, after having been used as such for over seven hundred years; and if we reckon from the time that Bishop Ecgred built the first church at Jedburgh, probably on the same site, we must add three centuries more. A thousand years form no unimportant portion of time, and during that period wonderful changes had taken place both as regards the physical aspect of the country and the social condition of its inhabitants. Great forests, in which roamed the wolf, the deer, and other wild animals, had disappeared; and large tracts of marshy ground and lochs of considerable extent, with which this country abounded, had given place to fields of waving grain. The chase had long since ceased to be the principal occupation of the inhabitants; the feudal system, which for centuries exercised a mighty influence upon society, had, as a civil institution, ceased to exist; and the unhappy wars between Scotland and England had come to an end by the union of the two countries under one sovereign. The people had been raised from a state of serfdom to one of freedom, from a condition of ignorance to one of enlightenment.

MINISTERS OF THE REFORMED CHURCH IN THE ABBEY.

PAUL METHVEN, formerly of Dundee, was nominated minister of Jedburgh by the Lords of the Congregation in 1560. In December 1562 John Knox was commissioned to come to Jedburgh to investigate into a serious charge of immorality against Methven, and on its being proved he was deposed and excommunicated. On his petition afterwards the General Assembly admitted him to repentance. Knox, in his *History of the Reformation in Scotland*, in alluding to the Methven case, says that there were appointed " certaine of the ministers to prescribe to him the forme of his declaration of repentance, which was thus in effect : First, That he should present himselfe bare-foot and bare-head, arayed in sack-cloth, at the principall entry of Saint Gyles Kirk in Edinburgh, at seven hours in the morning, upon the next Wednesday, and there to remain the space of an hour, the whole people beholding him, till the prayer was made, psalmes sung, and [the] text of Scripture was read, and then to come into the place appointed for expression of repentance, and tarry the time of sermon ; and to do likewise the next Friday following, and also upon the Sunday; and then, in the face of the whole church, to declare his repentance with his owne mouth. The same forme and manner he should use in Jedwart and Dundie ; and that being done, to present himself again at the next Generall Assembly following in winter, where he should be received to the communion of the Church. When the said Paul had received the said Ordinance, he took it very grievously, alleadging they had used over-great severity : Neverthelesse, being counselled and perswaded by divers notable personages, he began well in Edinburgh to proceed, whereby a great number were moved with compassion of his state ;

and likewise in Jedwart; but he left his duty in Dundie, and passing againe into England, the matter, not without offence to many, ceased."

Hill Burton, alluding to Methven's case, says: "Instead of any effort to conceal this reproach to their body [the Reformed clergy], they proclaimed it aloud as an awful and inscrutable judgment, and hunted the accused man until, whether guilty or not, he fled from his pursuers. He had a claim that would have served him well in any church disposed to hide the frailties of its zealous champions, for he had the glory of martyrdom. We find him outlawed in 1559 for 'usurping the authority and ministry of the Church,' and addressing large assemblies in Dundee and Montrose. The excitement aroused in a considerable body of men by the revelation among them of this one black sheep points to the conclusion that such sins were rare in the community to which Methven belonged" (*History of Scotland*). In a footnote Hill Burton adds: "Randolph, relating the scandal to Cecil as a morsel of important news, calls him 'a preacher brought up under Mr Coverdale'—the translator of the Bible we must suppose—and that 'he escaped into England, or was drowned in crossing the water thitherward.'"

ANDREW FORESTAR, translated from Liberton to Jedburgh in 1566, and thence to Tranent in 1568.

JOHN YOUNG, translated from Duns in 1569; translated to Irvine in Beltyne in 1570.

PETER CREICH, formerly of North Berwick, translated to Jedburgh in 1572.

ANDREW CLAYHILLIS, translated from Monifieth in 1574; translated to Eckford in 1593. "Andro Clayhillis, minister verbi Dei apud Jedburgh," witnesses the charter granted by Andrew, commendator of Jedburgh, to William Scott, Haughhead, previously referred to.

JOHN ABERNETHY, A.M., was elected minister of Jedburgh in 1593. He signed the protest against the introduction of Episcopacy on 1st July 1606; solicited the appointment to the archbishopric of Glasgow in 1615; was made D.D., and afterwards promoted to the bishopric of Caithness, retaining at the same time his charge in Jedburgh. In a synod held by him at Dornoch in 1623 it was decreed that every entering minister should pay the first year's stipend to the reparation and maintenance of that cathedral. He demitted his benefice in 1635, and was deposed from his bishopric by the Assembly of 1638. "By his writings," says Keith, "he appears a man of good literature." In a complimentary address by Dr John Strang, prefixed to the bishop's book, *Physicke for the Soule* (second edition, London, 1622), he is styled "virum multijuga eruditionis supellectile instructissimum." According to Scott's *Fasti*, he demitted his benefice before 15th September 1635, but in the articles given in to the presbytery of Jedburgh against Mr James Burnett in 1639, the parishioners "compleane of his [Burnett's] informall entrie, quho procured a presentation to the place not being vacant, but served at the tyme be a worthie man, Mr Jhon Abernethie, quho had nather dimitted the same nor was deposed thairfrom."

JAMES BURNETT, A.M., translated from Lauder in 1636. Presented by Charles I., and deposed in April 1639. In the process led against him by the presbytery the parishioners complained that he had intruded himself into the place without consent either of them or of the presbytery, and they stated that on the 4th of February 1636 Robert Simson, treasurer of the burgh of Jedburgh, procurator specially constituted in their name and behalf, passed to the personal presence of Mr James Burnett in the kirk of Jedburgh, and there protested that the said Mr James' presentation, collation, and present intended institution given to him thereupon, "suld be no wayes prejudiciall to the parochiners' libertie to oppose against any intrant minister to be imposed upon them without their consent."

WILLIAM JAMESON. On 15th April 1640 the heritors, elders, and others, "parishioners of the congregation of Jedburgh," desired the approbation and furtherance of the presbytery for planting Mr William Jameson, then minister at Longnewton,[1] at Jedburgh. The brethren received the supplication, and referred the full answer to the determination of the synod to be held the following week at Kelso. On the same day the Town Council ordained the magistrates, clerk, treasurer; John Rutherfurd of Bankend; John Rutherfurd, nottar; Adam Rutherfurd of the Hall; John Ainslie, chirurgeon; Andrew Rutherfurd, deacon; Adam Wilson, and James Forrest, "to ryd to the Assemblie at Kelso to supplicat for our minister, under paine of ten pounds ilk persone failzeir." On 12th June 1640 the presbytery, considering that Mr Jameson had been called by the heritors, parishioners, and burgh of Jedburgh to be minister at the kirk of Jedburgh, and that he had never acquainted them with the same, ordained their clerk to write presently in their name to the said Mr William, desiring him, in respect of the premises, and that the foresaid heritors, parishioners, and burgh desired a day to be appointed for receiving him, that he would be pleased to come to the presbytery that day eight days, that, knowing his own mind, they might with his consent appoint a day for receiving him at the foresaid kirk. On 17th June 1640 Mr Jameson declared to the presbytery that the heritors, parishioners, and burgh of Jedburgh had so far prevailed with him that, after their supplication to the presbytery granted, their act of transplantation obtained from the Provincial Assembly at Kelso in April 1640, and the urgent importunities of the foresaid persons to be their minister, and that "although he found himself for so great a charge altogether unable, yet to satisfy their godly desires, and to obey and serve God calling him thereunto, he had condescended to embrace the charge of the

---

[1] Maister William Jameson was provided to the "personage" of Longnewton, *jure devoluto*, by the archbishop of Glasgow, in default of Sir John Ker and his son, patrons, not presenting *debito tempore* (7th December 1622). Sir John was at that time *fugitans et lutitans*, being sometimes in Scotland and sometimes in England, "for eschewing of caption" (Haddington's *Decisions*, Vol. II.).

ministry at the kirk of Jedburgh." The presbytery fixed a day for receiving him, and on 24th June 1640 he was received as minister of Jedburgh, " in presence of, and with consent and applause of, the heritors, parishioners, and brough of Jedburgh, convened with the brethren for that effect." Mr Jameson was a staunch Presbyterian and a stern Covenanter. He was a member of six Assemblies before 1649, and of that of 1651. He died in 1661.

PETER BLAIR, A.M., translated from St Cuthbert's Second Charge in 1661. Presented by Charles II. Conformed to Episcopacy, and continued till 7th May 1673.

WILLIAM HUME, A.M., translated from Tinwald in 1674. Presented by Charles II. Deprived before 7th December for refusing the Test.

WILLIAM GALBREATH, A.M., translated from Morebattle in 1682. Presented by Charles II. Deprived by the Privy Council 29th August 1689 for not reading the Proclamation of the Estates, and not praying for William and Mary, but for James VII.

GABRIEL SEMPLE, A.M., translated from Kirkpatrick-Durham in 1690. He was the earliest of the field preachers, and had much influence among his brethren during the days of the persecution, and after the settlement of Church government. He died in August 1706. He had the character of being a prophet. Sir Walter Scott, in one of his notes to *Old Mortality*, states that Semple was one day passing the house of Kenmuir, to which workmen were making some additions, when he said to them, " Lads, you are very busy enlarging and repairing that house, but it will be burned like a crow's nest in a misty May morning," which accordingly came to pass, the house being burned by the English forces in a cloudy morning of May.

DANIEL M'KAY, formerly of Inveraray Second Charge, was translated to Jedburgh in 1707. Died September 1731.

JAMES ROWAT, translated from Dunlop in 1732. Presented by George II. Died June 1733.

JAMES WINCHESTER, A.M., translated from Elgin in 1734. In 1737 Mr Winchester offended many members of his congregation by reading the Porteous Act from the pulpit on the morning of a communion Sabbath. Several of them rose and left the church, observing as they did so that their minister had "celebrated the death of a murderer before the death of the Saviour" (*Two Centuries of Border Church Life*, by James Tait. Kelso, 1889). He died September 1755.

JOHN DOUGLAS, translated from Kenmore in 1758. He was a keen loyalist, and it is said that for his services during the rebellion of Prince Charles Stuart he received the new appointment. There was much opposition to his settlement in Jedburgh, which gave rise to a secession, afterwards called the Relief. He died in 1769.

JAMES MACKNIGHT, D.D., translated from Maybole in 1769. Presented by George III. Translated to Edinburgh in 1772. He was author of *The Harmony of the Four Gospels; The Truth of the Gospel History;* and *A New Translation of the Apostolical Epistles, with Commentary and Notes*. One of his hearers, on learning that the doctor was in Edinburgh in reference to *The Harmony of the Four Gospels*, remarked that he was making harmony among four evangelists who had never fallen out. He died in 1800.

THOMAS SOMERVILLE, translated from Minto in 1773. Presented by George III. Was made D.D. in 1787; historian of the reign of Queen Anne; one of His Majesty's Chaplains for Scotland. Died Father of the Church in 1830, in his ninetieth year. He was uncle and also father-in-law to the celebrated Mary Somerville, who was born in the manse of Jedburgh.

JOHN PURVES, translated from Lady Glenorchy's Chapel, Edinburgh, in 1830. Presented by William IV. Seceded with the Free Church in 1843. Was made LL.D. in 1875, and died in 1877.

GEORGE RITCHIE, A.M., translated from St Boswells in 1843. Was made D.D. in 1870, in which year he was Moderator of the General Assembly. He was the twentieth Protestant incumbent of the parish of Jedburgh, and the last who preached in Jedburgh Abbey Church. He demitted his charge in 1876, and died in Edinburgh in 1888.

REMOVAL OF THE CHURCH FROM THE ABBEY.

No time was lost between the opening of the new church and the commencement of the work in connection with the removal of the old church from the abbey, and Lord Lothian, being fully alive to the importance of this work, very wisely resolved to have it done under the superintendence of a skilled architect. It was accordingly placed under the care of Dr R. Rowand Anderson, Edinburgh, the architect who had so successfully restored the south doorway, as previously noticed. For the protection of the nave, it was, unfortunately, found necessary to place several tie beams across at the clerestory, which greatly mar the fine effect of the interior. The taking down of the modern masonry brought to light many curious and valuable specimens of the art of the carver, and of moulded stones formed hundreds of years ago by the hands of cunning workmen, but which by the vandals of the end of the eighteenth century were looked upon as only so much rubble, and used by them as such. The interest attached to their discovery was something akin to what a geologist would have experienced in disinterring a like number of fossils from some ancient formations, each specimen having a character peculiarly its own, and the period to which it belonged being quite easily ascertained. The comparative anatomist could with no greater certainty piece together the bones of an extinct animal than could these stones be assigned to their respective places in the ancient building. Many of them exhibited the chevron, the cable, dog-tooth, star, nail-head, and other ornaments, all belonging to the Transition Norman, which, there could be little doubt, formed part of the doorway that was taken down when a portion of the south aisle was removed in 1792. Then there were bases, capitals, at least one piscina; groin ribs, and various other mouldings, all of an early date. These have been preserved within the precincts of the abbey. The pillars and arches were scraped so as to free them from the paint and plaster that had disfigured them for nearly a century. No attempt was made to renew the capitals and arch mouldings that had been knocked away inside the old church, but in both of the side aisles the recently discovered groin ribs were replaced as far as practicable. The north wall was partially restored so as to indicate its original character, and the portion of the south wall that was wanting was rebuilt. Some of the pillars of the clerestory were renewed; nearly the whole of the corbelled eave course on the north was restored, and, to prevent water percolating down through the masonry, the wall-heads were covered with Caithness pavement. The wall-heads throughout the other parts of the building were carefully cleaned and covered with cement. On clearing away the accumulation of earth under the flooring of the church, the workmen came upon large quantities of human bones, all of which had been previously disturbed, and holes were dug in the adjoining grounds, where they were carefully deposited. One of the skulls picked up attracted some attention, as it bore the mark of what seemed to have been a wound caused by a sabre—the result doubtless of some dint given in the rough days of Border warfare—but the wound not being a fatal one had healed up before death gave the final stroke. They also came upon a regularly built vault of stone with arched roof, in the north aisle, containing two coffins, one of lead, the other of oak, and as all remembrance of the existence of these had been forgotten, many conjectures were made as to who were the occupants. The mystery was, however, cleared up. Thomas Philip Ainslie of Over Wells, in the parish of Jedburgh, having died at Newcastle on the 18th of May 1837, application was made to the kirk-session for permission to have his remains laid "in the vault within the church," granted by the heritors to his father. The kirk-session regretted that permission could not be granted—first, because the vault was originally formed to hold only the remains of "the late Mr Ainslie and his wife, both of whom were interred there, which filled up the whole space;" and second,

H

"because the place in which the vault is situated, which was formerly a passage, now forms part of the place of public worship, having been some time ago taken in and seated" (*Minute of Session*). Several Scottish copper coins belonging to the reigns of Mary Queen of Scots, Charles I., and Charles II. were also come upon, and these were claimed by the Crown as treasure-trove. We may mention here that in 1849, when some repairs were made on the abbey, there was found a leaden seal, which had been attached to a papal Bull of Pope Gregory IX. On one side were the words "GREGORIVS : PP : VIIII," and on the other "SPASPE," under which were two heads, believed to represent those of St Peter and St Paul. This seal is now in the Jedburgh Museum. A seal of Pope Innocent III. was found at Friars' Bank some years ago, and is now in the possession of the Marquess of Lothian. These both belong to the first half of the thirteenth century. The first mentioned is somewhat of an oval shape, while the other is round or circular. Up till the thirteenth century such seals were suspended by means of silk threads or a slip of parchment, but after that date they were generally attached to the document itself. From time to time, during excavations in the abbey, several interesting articles have been found, including a gold ring that was presented to Sir Walter Scott, pieces of molten brass—doubtless the result of one or other of the burnings—fragments of the old abbey glass, and an antique key figured on the opposite page.

The appearance of the west front of the abbey has been somewhat changed by the removal of a mullion and transom from the centre window. The mullion branched away near the top, and formed two pointed lights; and the transom, which had rudely-formed cusps, crossed it half-way up. There is good reason for believing that originally the window was not so divided, and this statement is supported by the fact that while the chamfer or splay at the sides of the window is small, that at the top, beginning with the arch, is much larger. The stones with the large chamfer agreed with the mullion, and were in all likelihood put in at the same time. No doubt Billings gives something like what may be called

Antique Key found in Jedburgh Abbey.

a representation of a restoration of the west front of the abbey, and in this window he places a mullion and transom. The transom, however, as given in his illustration, is much more artistic than that which it was intended to represent; and it must be further observed that he places mouldings at the sides of the window where such never existed, and makes them run into the cusps of the transom, as if the latter naturally formed part of them. Above the window, on the north side of the doorway, there was a small window with a trefoil arch, which was removed in consequence of its having been inserted there at a late date—probably when the church was fitted up in the west end. It seemed to have belonged to the fourteenth or fifteenth century, and must have originally occupied a place in a different part of the abbey. An interesting view of the west front of the abbey is given in Grose's *Antiquities of Scotland,* Vol. I., p. 131, published in 1789, and reproduced in the present work (see opposite page). The great west window seems at that time to have been glazed in the lower half, with shutters to protect the glass. No mullion is seen. The window to the right of the great doorway had been converted into an entrance to one of the galleries, and a few steps are seen leading up to it. At the top of this strange-looking entrance are seen a few panes of glass. On examination it will be seen that the wall under the window had been cut down for some little distance below the string-course, the better to adapt it to its new purpose. At the corresponding window on the other side of the great doorway the illustration shows a few panes of glass at the top, the remainder of this window being built up.

But there were other parts of the fabric that required serious attention. The tower, on the north side, was found to be in a very unsafe condition, and something required to be done for its preservation. The danger was not a thing of yesterday, for, as we have already seen, one of the "pryme pillars" was in a dangerous state as early as 1636. The frailty of this "pryme pillar" had not a little to do with the resolution to leave the church under the tower for that at the west end of the nave; and for the same reason it was found necessary at a later date not to remove the whole of the old walls. Lord Lothian at one time seriously considered the propriety of renewing the north piers so as to give the tower a further lease of stability, but ultimately the idea was departed from, and means were taken to preserve it as far as possible in its present state. A brick buttress was thrown up against the north-west pier, which bulged out considerably, and large wooden beams were placed against the north-east pier—doubtless the "pryme pillar" already alluded to—which is almost wholly encased in rude masonry. To lighten the top of the north wall a belfry was taken down, and this lightened the weakest part by about 150 tons of masonry. The belfry consisted of three distinct parts, namely, a central octagonal tower, which rose twenty feet above the wall-head, and an open bellcot on each side. The belfry formed no part of the original design of the tower, as was easily determined by an examination of the architectural features of the different portions. The date of its erection cannot, however, be ascertained with any degree of certainty. The octagonal part was clearly of first Transition character, of about the same age as the pointed part of the choir, and therefore at least two hundred years older than the tower on which it stood. The probability is that it was one of the turrets of the eastern gable (its measurements were such as to support this idea), and that it was erected on the tower shortly after the abbey sustained the destructive injuries at the hands of the English in 1544-45.

From these injuries, as we have seen, the monastery never recovered, and it would seem that, instead of the whole of the church being afterwards occupied, only a portion under the tower was fitted up for worship, this being used by Roman Catholics, Presbyterians, and Episcopalians successively until 1671, when the last-named body removed to the west end of the nave. If our idea is correct, the belfry was erected on the top of the tower for the use of the church under it. The kirk clock was fitted up in the centre turret, and the bells were suspended in the bellcots at the sides. Previous to this, the clock had occupied a position on the north side of the tower, where the mark of its dial is still seen at the centre opening, and the abbey bells had evidently been hung in the upper storey. The lower portion of the stair leading to the tower would seem to have been put up also for the use of this church, and may have been part of one of the east turret stairs. It is in the south transept, in a position where such a thing could not have originally been intended, but quite suitable for this church, as may be seen from the fragments of its walls that still remain. We have seen an old painting of the abbey, showing the south wall of this church rising to near the vaulted roof of the transept. There was a window pretty well up. The lower portion of this wall still exists, and crosses the transept from the foot of the stair to a pier on the west side.

Besides the work we have already mentioned as having been done under the direction of Dr Anderson, concrete was laid round the foundations of all the lower pillars to prevent a subsidence; and to add to the appearance of the north transept a large quantity of earth—the accumulation of ages—was cleared from its base. No cost was spared to improve the amenity of the abbey, and with this view the manse, which was close by, and several other houses, were taken down. The whole work, as may well be imagined, was one of great labour and expense; but the result has been such as to make Jedburgh Abbey one of the most beautiful ecclesiastical ruins in Scotland, and for this the Marquess of Lothian deserves the gratitude—which he will no doubt receive—of all lovers of architectural art. To give some idea of the great work carried out by his lordship for the improvement of the abbey—including the erection of the new church and manse—we may state that the cost has been estimated at not less than £20,000. In addition to all this, we have reason to believe that Lord Lothian has in contemplation the restoration of the dilapidated portions of the west doorway, as well as of the attached arcade at the sides of the great west window.

same pitch, as may be seen by the mark on the east wall of the tower.

But what about the lower marking? That it cannot be the mark of an inner roof, as some have suggested, is clearly proved by the fragments of a water-tablet, or drip-stone, which still remain in some of the cuttings on both sides of the nave, immediately above where this roof would join the wall; and also by the marking on the south wall of the tower, a little above the stone-vaulted roof of the transept, and which crosses an opening there in the same way as the lower marking on the west. It must therefore have been an outer one; but when could a new roof be rendered necessary? When the ends of the timber became decayed, it was not unusual to cut off the decayed parts and lower the roof. In the case of Jedburgh Abbey, however, much more was done than the mere lowering, for along the whole length of the nave two cuttings—one for resting the top of the side aisle roof, and the other for the insertion of a drip-stone to throw off the water—have been made just at the spring of the including arches of the triforium, and this would necessitate the filling up of the subdividing arches in some way, but whether by windows or otherwise the effect would be anything but pleasing.

Regarding the central roof of the nave matters are no less puzzling. The lower roof had crossed an opening in the under storey of the tower in the same way, a portion of the arch having been left outside; and it must also have crossed the St Catherine's wheel at the west end, unless by some peculiar arrangement it was raised at that part. We can find another reason than the decay of the timber here that necessitated a change. In 1523—probably within thirty years of the erection of the former roof—the abbey was burned by the English under the Earl of Surrey, after a whole day's cannonading, and at that time, we suspect, the nave and its aisles were rendered roofless.

As there are no double roof-marks on the east and north sides of the tower, we may naturally infer that the chancel and north transept did not share the same fate as the nave at the date mentioned. It seems strange that in repairing the damage done by this destructive burning, the roofs were not put up on the old lines, but in a position that entailed greater labour, and which must have spoiled all æsthetic effect.

The next visits of the "auld enemies" were in 1544-45, when the whole abbey was so sadly wrecked that no attempt was made to restore it, the canons contenting themselves with erecting a place under the tower for the carrying on of worship. The remains of this erection, which have come down to our day, are rude enough to show either that the taste of the canons had by that time become very much debased, or, what is more likely, that they had then no heart to restore their church to anything like its former beauty, a church that had undergone many vicissitudes, and which was before long likely to undergo more. The thunder notes of the coming Reformation had been already heard, and were becoming louder and louder at the nearer approach of the storm.

MASONS' MARKS ON THE ABBEY.

FROM very early times it had been the practice of individual masons to distinguish their work by their own particular marks. These marks or symbols are to be found on the Pyramids of Egypt, on the walls of the Temple at Jerusalem, on the altars and other works of the ancient Romans, and on all the mediæval ecclesiastical structures in this country and on the Continent. They have been detected also in India, on the walls of the fortress of Allahabad, which was erected in 1542. "These marks," says the late Dr John Alexander Smith, one of the secretaries of the Society of Antiquaries of Scotland, in a paper on this subject (see *Transactions*, Vol. IV.), "vary much in character and shape, but may be all included in two classes—the false or blind mark of the apprentice, displaying an equal number of points; and the true mark of the fellow-craft or passed mason, which always consists of an unequal number of points. Two marks not unfrequently occur on the same stone, showing that it had been hewn by the apprentice, and finished or passed as correct by the mason, who places on it his own distinctive mark." Considerable interest has been shown during recent years regarding these marks, and various theories have been advanced concerning them. In a paper "On Certain Marks Discoverable on the Stones of various Buildings Erected in the Middle Ages," Mr G. Godwin says: "The fact that in these buildings it is only a certain number of stones which bear symbols; that the marks found in different countries (although the variety is great) are in many cases identical, and in all have a singular accordance in character, seems to show that the men who employed them did so by system, and that the system, if not the same in England, Germany, and France, was closely analogous in one country to that of the others." A good deal has been written about the symbolic significance of these marks, but to little purpose. They seem to us rather to have had a practical aim than to have had any mystery attached to them.

"Masonic tradition informs us," says Mackey, in his *Lexicon of Freemasonry,* "that, at the building of King Solomon's Temple, every mason was provided with a peculiar mark, which he placed upon his work to distinguish it from that of his fellows. By the aid of these marks the overseers were enabled without difficulty to trace any piece of defective work to the faulty workman, and every chance of imposition, among so large an assemblage of craftsmen as were engaged at the Temple, was thus effectually prevented." Masonic associations or guilds existed in Rome in the time of the Emperors. In the tenth century they were established in Lombardy, in which they reared many churches, and afterwards passed into all the countries of Christendom. They received encouragement from popes, who granted them privileges peculiar to themselves. A monopoly was granted to them for the erection of all religious edifices; they were declared independent of the sovereigns in whose dominions they might be temporarily residing; they could regulate the amount of their wages, and were exempt from all kinds of taxation (*Lexicon of Freemasonry,* third edition).

We may mention as a somewhat curious incident that on removing a small portion of the old wall of the south aisle of the nave of the abbey there was found a piece of a string-course with the markings of the tool still fresh and distinct as when it was chiselled six hundred years ago. It had been spoiled in the working, and rejected in consequence. The stone had been intended to be a corner-piece, but, to use a technical term, the workman had "cut its throat." The workman and his name had long since been forgotten, but the stone bearing his distinctive mark still bore testimony against him. Never did fossil taken from the rock tell its story more clearly.

Dr Daniel Wilson, in his learned work on the *Archæology and Prehistoric Annals of Scotland,* while alluding to the same subject, observes on pp. 640-1: "The observation and collation of these marks have accordingly become objects of interest, as calculated to aid in the elucidation of the history of the mediæval masonic guilds. . . . Many of the subordinate lines added to regular figures are still recognised among the craft as additions given to distinguish the symbols of two masons when the mark of a member admitted from another lodge was the same as that already borne by one of their own number. If the entire series, or the greater number of the marks on one building, could be detected on another apparently of the same age, it would be such a coincidence as could hardly be ascribed to any other cause than that both were the work of the same masonic lodge. . . . The united co-operation of a very few zealous labourers may soon bring such a question to the test, if sufficient care is taken to discriminate between the original work and the additions or alterations of subsequent builders."

As a contribution to the materials for the elucidation of this interesting subject, we give on the opposite page a series of marks found on Jedburgh Abbey, noting at the same time the portions of the building on which they occur, and the periods to which they belong. Dr Smith gives, among many others, illustrations of a number of marks on Jedburgh Abbey, but the list now given will be found to be much more complete. The marks are here arranged under the following heads: I. On Early Norman work, in choir, on portions of original transepts, and piers of same date; II. Norman Transition work, on west gable, nave, and original portion of south wall; III. Fourteenth or Fifteenth Century Decorated, on north transept; IV. End of Fifteenth Century, on the tower and south piers of the tower.

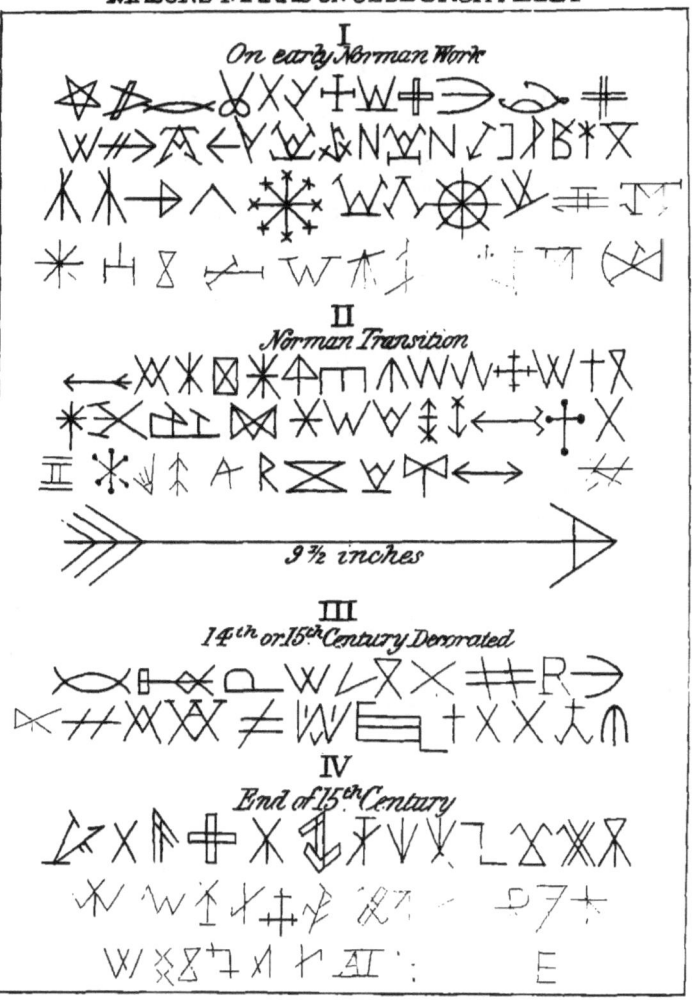

MEASUREMENTS OF THE ABBEY CHURCH.

	Feet.	In.
Extreme length over walls,	235	0
Length of interior of nave,	129	0
Crossing of tower,	34	0
Length of choir,	58	0
Extreme length inside the walls,	218	0
Width of nave between centre of piers,	27	6
Width of north aisle from centre of pier,	15	2
Width of south aisle from centre of pier,	14	2
North transept projects from centre of tower,	68	0
Width of north transept outside the walls,	32	4
Height of wall-head of north transept,	39	2
Height of wall-head of nave from floor,	49	3
Height of tower to wall-head,	86	0
Piers of nave from centre to centre,	14	0
West doorway, height at ingoing,	14	$4\frac{1}{2}$
,, width at ingoing,	6	$1\frac{1}{2}$
,, recessed,	6	2
,, height at outermost order,	21	2
,, width at outermost order,	20	4
West window, height,	18	10
,, width,	5	8
St Catherine's wheel, diameter within circular moulded order,	9	4
Windows at side of west doorway, height,	9	2
,, ,, ,, width,	2	5
Great window in north transept, height,	28	2
,, ,, ,, width,	9	8

MEASUREMENTS OF THE ABBEY CHURCH.

	Feet.	In.
Side windows in north transept, height,	16	0
„ „ „ width,	5	6
Windows in clerestory of nave, height,	8	0
„ „ „ width,	1	8
Windows in clerestory of choir, height,	8	8½
„ „ „ width,	2	11
Windows below clerestory of choir, a jamb of two of which only remains, height (probable),	17	0
„ „ width,	3	2½
South Norman doorway, height at ingoing,	10	6
„ „ width at ingoing,	4	8
„ „ recessed,	3	1½
„ „ height at outermost order,	13	8
„ „ width at outermost order,	11	0

Anglo Saxon Cross — Jedburgh Abbey.

SCULPTURED STONES IN THE ABBEY.

IN the north transept of the abbey are preserved three very fine specimens of early sculpture, but, unfortunately, none of them is entire. The one most elaborately carved represents a tree, the branches of which form circles, and in these are two birds and four nondescript animals, three of them being shown as eating the fruit of the tree, and one of them gnawing a branch. This stone was at one time built in as a lintel above the south aisle of the choir, but several years ago the present writer pointed it out to the Rev. Canon Greenwell of Durham, and shortly afterwards it was removed to where it now is. Mr Greenwell pronounced it to be part of an Anglo-Saxon cross belonging to about the ninth century. It was afterwards figured in Stuart's *Sculptured Stones of Scotland* (see Vol. II., plate xxviii., with relative notice). Regarding the removal of this stone from its original place in the abbey, Mr Stuart says: "This stone figured on this plate was recently brought to my notice by my friend, the Rev. William Greenwell of Durham. It was built into the south aisle of the chancel as a lintel of an opening, but at my request it was removed from the wall by the kind permission of the Marquess of Lothian, for the purpose of obtaining a correct drawing of it, and it is now placed in the north transept." "At the church of Norham, which Ecgred built, there were," says Mr Stuart, "many crosses of Anglo-Saxon character. The cross at Jedburgh seems undoubtedly to be of the same period, and must be classed with similar remains found at Abercorn, Norham, Coldingham, Lindisfarne, Jarrow, and Hexham, all sites of Saxon foundation." The two other stones in the transept are figured in the same work, and are believed to belong to the same period.

Another cross, archaic in character, and retaining the typical features of the Celtic form, is built in as a lintel in a recess over the south chapel of the choir, and under the stair leading to the tower.

The stone has raised border fillets, but the cross has no ornament by which its date can be determined. The wall into which it has been built is twelfth-century work, and the cross is probably of about the same date. Possibly the stone may have got broken after it had been worked, and then been built in as a lintel. The dotted lines indicate the hidden portion resting on the jamb of the opening.

There is another stone of much interest, figured below, which was long a puzzle to archæologists, built in as a lintel at the foot of the north-west turret stair. It was known to bear a Roman inscription, and a few contracted words could be made out, but it was never successfully deciphered till 1885. In that year the Marquess of

Lothian caused a cast to be taken and forwarded to the Rev. Dr J. Collingwood Bruce, Newcastle, who contributed a paper on the subject to the Berwickshire Naturalists' Club. He gives the inscription as it appeared on the cast with its three leaf stops, and is of opinion that it ought to be expanded as follows:—

I[OVI] O[PTIMO] M[AXIMO] VEXI-
LLATIO RETORVM GAESA-
[TORVM] Q[VORVM] G[VRAM]
A[GEBAT] IVL[IVS]
SEVER[INVS] TRIB[VNVS]

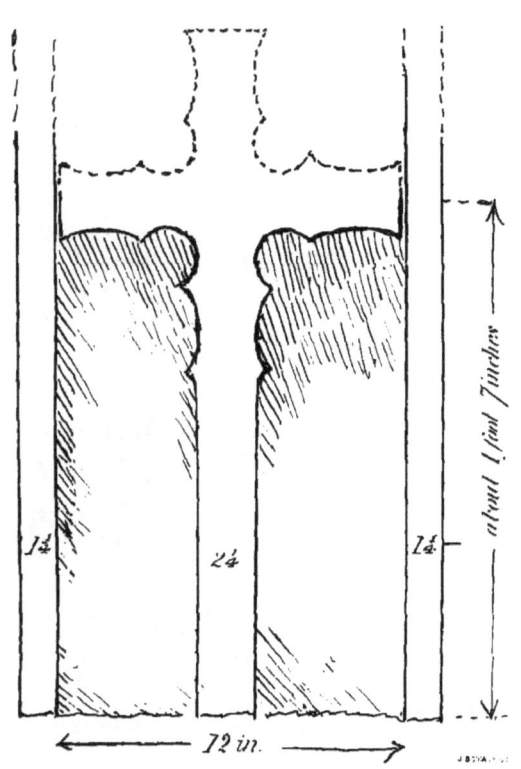

Scale 2 inches equal to 1 foot.

ANCIENT CROSS NOW F... ...ING
IN JEDBURGH ABBEY.

This he translates as follows :—" To Jupiter, the best and greatest, the Vexillation of Rhætian spearmen, under the command of Julius Severinus the tribune [dedicate this altar]." Dr Bruce thinks there must have been a line or two more on the inscription, which had been chipped off by the builders of the abbey. At all events, he says, there would be the usual termination V. S. L. M. (" votum solvit libens merito "). He had always understood a *vexillation* to be a body of men selected from different cohorts, but fighting under one common *vexillum* or standard, and sent on some special expedition. *Retorum* he regards as the rustic spelling for Rhætorum. The Rhætians came from the Alps, and were named Gæsati, from their being armed with the *gæsum*, a kind of spear or javelin. At Risingham, near Woodburn, in the north of Northumberland, was found a stone with an inscription which mentions the *Reti* Gæsati, and as that place is situated upon Watling Street, and Jedburgh only two miles from this Roman road, it would be an easy thing, as Dr Bruce remarks, for the Rhæti Gesati to find their way from Risingham to Jedburgh (*Proceedings of the Berwickshire Naturalists' Club*, 1884, Appendix).

NOTABLE PERSONS BURIED IN THE ABBEY.

It is not a little remarkable that of all the abbots, priors, and canons of this monastery who must have been buried within its sacred precincts, not one of their graves can now be pointed out. Not a few of them were great men in their time, wielding mighty influence in the state, as well as within their own ecclesiastical jurisdiction; but their power and sacerdotal pomp are things of the past, and they have gone down to unknown graves, like the meanest serf or the poorest peasant. It is literally true of them that the place that once knew them knoweth them no more. Their beautiful house has been cast down, not one stone standeth upon another; and their ruined church shall no more resound with the matin song or the vesper hymn.

> "Thou unrelenting past!
> Strong are the barriers round thy dark domain,
> And fetters sure and fast
> Hold all that enter thy unbreathing reign."

The first person of whom there is any account as having been buried in the church of Jedburgh is one Eadulf, a younger son of the Earl of Northumberland, who was interred here about the end of the eleventh century. But he was not permitted to rest undisturbed. He had, it seems, been one of the assassins of Bishop Walcher, a priest of Lorraine, who had received an appointment from William the Conqueror, and though he had met his own death at the hands of a woman, and was laid quietly at rest within the church, his body was cast out from thence as execrable—"*talis spurcitia*" are the words of Simeon of Durham—by Turgot, the prior and archdeacon of Durham. What afterwards became of the bones of the unfortunate Eadulf we are not told.

Gordon, in his *Scotichronicon*, says that John Achaius, the preceptor, chaplain, and intimate friend of David I., was buried here. It was by his advice that the Canons Regular were brought from France to Jedburgh. He was consecrated bishop of Glasgow by Pope Paschal II., with consent of Archbishop Thurstin of York, who, as well as some of his successors, claimed metropolitical jurisdiction over Southern Scotland. John, who was of a restless and energetic character, bold in action and undaunted in spirit, refused submission to the see of York, in defiance of the mandates of three successive popes, and rather than yield to pope or prelate, he abdicated his see, and retired into a convent of Benedictines in France. He had previously made a pilgrimage to Jerusalem, where he resided for some time. In 1138 an assembly of clergy and barons was held in Carlisle, when it was resolved to send a messenger to France with letters from the legate to the effect that if he did not return sentence would pass against him (R. Hagustald; see note in Hale's *Annals of Scotland*). But he cared nothing for the legate, the clergy, or the barons—Pope Innocent II. called him "ipso multum resistente"— and it was only the mandate of his own king that brought him back. He died bishop of Glasgow in May 1147, according to Gordon, having been connected with that see for thirty-two years.

IN THE CHOIR.—THE RUTHERFURDS.

On 13th July 1464 the abbot of Jedburgh granted a right of burial in the abbey to Robert Rutherfurd of Chatto and his wife. The grant was in these terms: " Be it kend till almen be thir presents letteris, Ws, Andrew, throw the grace off God, Abbot of ye Abbay of Jedworth, with consent and assent of our halle convent till haff grantyt, and be thir present letteris grantis til our weylbelufyt Robert off Rudirfurd and Chattow, and Margaret, hys wyff, thar laris within the quher of our Abbay of Jedworth, in the mydlis of the sam nixt the utmost grese [steps] quhar ye lectern standis, quhen that God wesys tham to pass off this warlde, and to la thar throioch quhen it plessis tham in ye sayd place. For ye quhylk laris in ye said quher we grant ws fulley content and payit. In witness of ye quhylk thingis we haff set the common sell of our Abbay till thir present letteris at the sayd Abbay of Jedworth, this xiii day of ye moneth of July in the zher off God a thousand four hundreth sixty and four zheris, befoir thir witness, Dene Phelip Waleyss, superior of our Closter, Dene Walter Mol, Dene Walter Pyle, Dene Johne Cant, Dene Alexander Geddes, Dene Henry off Glasgow, Dene Wylliam of Jedworth, and Dene James of Dryburgh, Channonis of our sayd Abbay, and divers vthers " (*The Rutherfurds of that Ilk*).

Curiously enough, the seal appended to this document—a facsimile of which is given in the Rutherfurd Book—is *not* the seal of the abbey, but that of Cardinal David Beaton, and may be seen described in Henry Laing's *Catalogue*, Vol. I., No. 884. Dr David Dickson, of the Register House, Edinburgh, has an excellent cast from a particularly clear impression of this seal. How a seal which could not have existed before December 1538—the date when Beaton was made a cardinal—became connected with a grant of July 1464, it would be interesting to know. It is no business of ours to attempt to explain; we simply call attention to the fact.

The whole of the choir was afterwards divided among the Rutherfurds as their resting-place, and allotments assigned for those of Edgerston, Hunthill, Hundalee, Fernington, Bankend, the Hall, the Townhead, to the Lorimer, and to the Bailie and his son. The reason given for the ancestors of Robert Rutherfurd of Fernilee not being buried in the choir, but in the Bell House Brae (north-west part of the churchyard), is that when the English made one of their raids upon Jedburgh they carried off the largest bell belonging to the abbey, which hung in the tower on the slope above referred to, and that Richard Rutherfurd, having pursued them with a handful of men, made a desperate effort to recover it, but was overpowered and mortally wounded, and requested to be buried in the Bell House. Robert Rutherfurd of Fernilee, who was a writer in Edinburgh, and Deputy Receiver General of Supply of Scotland, was the last of his family who was buried in the Bell House, where his son erected a monument for him, with the coat of arms of the family (*The Rutherfurds of that Ilk*). Tradition says that the bell was carried off to Hexham. The Bell House has long since been removed, but the oldest family of the Jedburgh Rutherfords still bury on the site.

The Rutherfurds were an ancient and powerful clan, and several of them, including the Lairds of Edgerston, Hundalee, and Hunthill, were present at the Raid of the Reidswire in 1575. Richard Rutherfurd of Littleheuch, son of the "Cock of Hunthill," at that time provost of Jedburgh, led on the burghers, who came upon the scene while the skirmish was going on, and raising their slogan, "A Jedworth! A Jedworth!" turned the tide of battle in favour of their countrymen. An old ballad in reference to this says:—

> "Bauld Rutherfurd he was fu' stout,
> Wi' his nine sons him round about,
> He led the town of Jedward out;
> All bravely fought that day."

A flat tombstone of some interest in the north-west part of the choir lay for many years in a dilapidated condition, but has now been restored. It is believed to be that of John Rutherfurd of Bankend, and of his wife, Barbara Gledstanes, daughter of James Gledstanes of Cocklaw and that Ilk. John Rutherfurd was Sheriff-Depute of Roxburghshire and Commissioner to Parliament in 1619. The stone bears the initials "M. I. R." and "B. G." and the date 1636. Round the border of the stone is the following Latin inscription:— "CHRISTO : BEATOS : FIRMA : NECTIT : COPULA : QUOS : ATRA : MORS : A : MUNDO : DIVULSERAT"—"A firm link binds to Christ the blessed whom black death had torn from the world."

John Rutherfurd of Mossburnford, who is alluded to by the poet Burns in his *Border Tour*, is buried in the north-east of the choir. When fifteen years of age he went to America, and after his arrival at Detroit he went with Captain Robson of the 77th Regiment on an exploring expedition, and was taken captive by the natives, with whom he lived for some time till he managed to make his escape. He afterwards served thirty years in the 42nd Highlanders, in which corps he held the rank of ensign, and was engaged in South America. He was afterwards appointed major in the Dumfries Militia, and died in Jedburgh on 12th July 1830, at the age of eighty-four. The major wrote an interesting sketch of his captivity among the North American Indians.

The last man of note who was buried in the choir was John Rutherfurd of Edgerston, who did much for the good of his native county, and in respect for his memory a beautiful Gothic monument was erected by public subscription. The inscription upon it gives the true character of this highly-esteemed county gentleman, and is as follows:—" To the memory of John Rutherfurd, Esq. of Edgerston, Vice-Lieutenant-Colonel of the Local Militia, and for two successive parliaments knight of the shire for the county of Roxburgh. A gentleman distinguished alike by eminent talents and unshaken integrity, who during a long and useful life devoted his exertions to the maintenance of order in the country at large, and to the promotion of every local improvement in his native district. Zealous in the performance of his public duties, just and correct in every private relation; a loyal subject, a considerate landlord, he left an example of public spirit and private worth, and of the true dignity of an independent Scottish gentleman. Died 6th May 1834, aged 86." He was married to Mary Ann Leslie, daughter of General the Honourable Alexander Leslie, son of the Earl of Leven. General Leslie and his wife, the Honourable Rebecca Leslie, are also interred here, on the south side of the choir.

There is a tombstone on the south side, in the Fernington allotment, in memory of a daughter of the house of Riddell, with the following inscription:—

"Here lyes a religious and virtuous gentlewoman, Jean Riddell, daughter of Sir Andrew Riddell of that Ilk, who died in the Lord in the year of God MDCLX., and of her age 80.

> She lived a holy life,
> To Christ resigned her breath;
> Her soul is now with God
> Triumphing over death."

In the North Transept.—The Kers.

At what time the north transept was set apart as the burial-place of the Kers of Ferniherst we have not the means of ascertaining. The tombstone which bears the oldest date is that of Sir Andrew Ker, but the date—1524—is wrong. He was appointed Bailie of Jedburgh Forest in November 1542, at which time he was not a knight, and a writer in the *Genealogist* says he was not knighted till after January 1543. Sir Andrew, who was a man of courage and ability, was Warden of the Middle Marches of Scotland, and one of the commissioners appointed to treat for peace with England. For his services to the country he was rewarded with the barony of Oxnam. When Ferniherst was captured by the English in 1523 he was taken prisoner, but soon regained his liberty, and the same year he commanded 4000 Scots and French at the storming of Wark Castle. He died in 1545.

Sir John Ker, Warden of the Marches, also lies here. He did good service against the English. The writer in the *Genealogist* says that John was knighted in 1548, but this is inconsistent with the statement made by Bishop Lesly in his *History* that he was, along with other Border chiefs, knighted by the Lord Governor on the occasion of the consecration in the abbey of Jedburgh of David Panter as bishop of Ross in 1552. Sir John was father of the famous Sir Thomas Ker, Warden of the Marches, Provost of Edinburgh and Jedburgh, who suffered many trials for his zeal in the cause of the unfortunate Queen Mary, and having died in ward in Aberdeen in 1586, he was buried before the communion table there. Sir John died in 1562. On the tombstone the date is 1559.

Sir Andrew Ker, eldest son of the above Sir Thomas, received a charter under the Great Seal in 1587 confirming him in the office of Heritable Bailie of Jedburgh Abbey lands, held by his father, grandfather, and great-grandfather. He was a Gentleman of the Bedchamber to James VI. in 1591. He was provost of Jedburgh in 1601, when a fight took place in the burgh between the Kers of Ferniherst and the Turnbulls, when Thomas Ker of Crailing, Robert

Turnbull of Bewlie, and John Middlemast were killed and several persons wounded. Sir Andrew as provost of the burgh arrested the murderers of his brother, one of whom was capitally punished, but he, his brother James, James Ker of Lyntellie, and others of their kinsmen and followers, were brought to trial the same year for the slaughter and demembration of those who suffered on the other side. The Earl of Angus, as lord of the regality of Jedburgh, claimed the right to try Sir Andrew and the others as dwelling within his regality; the king's advocate denied this, but it was proved that Ferniherst lay within the regality. He then alleged that Sir Andrew, as provost of a royal burgh, could not be repledged, and eventually Lord Angus withdrew his claim of jurisdiction, except as regards James Ker of Lyntellie and his son, but under protest; the case was delayed and apparently never pursued as against the Kers. On 2nd February 1622 he was raised to the peerage with the title of Baron Jedburgh, and died in 1631 without any surviving male issue. His tombstone is seen under the great window, and on the wall over it are his arms, on a shield a chevron bearing three mullets, the supporters being two savages, and the motto, "Forward in the name of God."

Sir James Ker of Crailing, who married the heiress of James Rutherfurd of Hundalee, also lies here. He was brother to the first Lord Jedburgh. Sir James, then designated of Hundalee, represented the county of Roxburgh in Parliament in 1630. He died in 1645, and his son,

Robert Ker of Crailing and Hundalee, having become heir male of Ferniherst, had, on 11th July 1670, the title of Baron Jedburgh confirmed. His lordship married Christian, daughter of Sir Alexander Hamilton of Innerwick, and, having no family, he got an extended patent to include the nearest male line, descended from his great-granduncle, Robert Ker of Ancrum, youngest son of the ninth Laird of Ferniherst, and the Ancrum Kers, on coming into possession, added a second "r" to the family name to distinguish them from the Cessford family. Lord Robert died in August 1692. The title and entailed estate of Ferniherst, and the estate of Hundalee, eventually fell to the Lothian family, who holds three peerages, including that of Ancram. Both Robert Lord Jedburgh and Lady Christian are interred here, and their arms are quartered on the tombstone. His lordship, perhaps thinking that no more burials would take place in the transept, made a testament on 4th November 1688, by which he mortified a thousand merks Scots "for upholding the ylle [aisle] of Pherniherst." He seems also to have built the dividing wall between the Ferniherst aisle and that of the Turnbull's, which adjoins it. Over the entrance are his arms and initials, with the date 1681.

There is a stone in the transept with the initials "M. K.," and the date 1658, but it is not in its original place. It was found in another part of the abbey and put up here a number of years ago. The stone is probably that of Mark Ker of Dolphinston.

On the 12th of July 1870 the remains of William Schomberg Robert Kerr, eighth Marquess of Lothian, were interred here, it being, we believe, his lordship's wish to rest within the precincts of the abbey he loved so well; and in 1879 a suitable monument to his memory was erected over his tomb. This monument, the workmanship of Mr G. F. Watts, R.A., London, is of Caen stone, and shows a recumbent figure of the late marquess. The likeness is an excellent one, and a fine feeling of repose pervades the whole. He was a nobleman of very refined tastes and high literary ability, and was author of an able work on the Civil War in America entitled *The Confederate Secession*. His lordship was the founder of the Lothian Historical Prize in the University of Oxford, and with him originated the scheme of removing from the abbey the parish church which for centuries disfigured the beautiful fabric.

IN THE CHOIR CHAPELS.

The south aisle of the choir was long used as the burial-place of the ministers of the parish, and here lies the Rev. Thomas Somerville, D.D., F.R.S.E., senior chaplain-in-ordinary to the king, and author of the *History of the Reign of Queen Anne, My Own Life and Times*, and other works. He was minister of the parish for fifty-seven years, and was uncle and father-in-law to the celebrated Mary Somerville. On his visit to Jedburgh the poet Burns was introduced to Dr Somerville, who, he says, was "a man and a gentleman, but sadly addicted to punning." On the appearance of this passage in Dr Currie's Memoir of the poet, Dr Somerville entirely abandoned the practice. It may be stated that the doctor's daughter Margaret, who is also interred here, was the first love of Sir David Brewster (see *Home Life of Sir David Brewster*, by Mrs Gordon).

The last who was buried in this chapel was the Rev. Dr John Purves, who was minister of the parish from 1830 till the Disruption in 1843, when he joined the Free Church. He was a popular preacher, and a volume of his sermons was published in 1846. He died in October 1877.

In the railed enclosure on the south of the choir, which marks the site of the south chapel, lie the remains of Archibald Jerdon, an ardent and successful student of ornithology and botany. He was the son of Mr A. Jerdon of Bonjedward, where he was born in September 1819. Some of his notices of birds are contained in the earlier volumes of the *Zoologist*. He devoted much attention to the study of cryptogamic plants, and made a collection of ferns, lichens, and mosses. He contributed a "List of Fungi observed in the Neighbourhood of Jedburgh" to the *Proceedings of the Berwickshire Naturalists' Club*. In the course of his rambles he discovered several species new to science, as well as others which had not been previously detected in Britain. Two species were named in honour of himself, one of which was *Sphæria Jerdoni*. He died at Allerton House, Jedburgh, in January 1874.

UNDER THE TOWER.

Under the tower, and near to the north-east pier, lie the remains of the Rev. Thomas Boston (son of the Rev. Thomas Boston, author of *The Fourfold State*), the first minister of the Relief Congregation in Jedburgh, and one of the founders of that body. Previous to this he was minister of the parish of Oxnam, and his becoming a Dissenter was, according to some, more the result of pet than of principle. On the death of Mr Winchester, minister of Jedburgh in 1755, a presentation to the vacancy was obtained by the Marquess of Lothian from the Crown in favour of Mr Bonar, minister of Cockpen; but this was resisted successfully by the Jedburgh Town Council, and Mr Douglas, Kenmore, got the living after much opposition. A strong party was in favour of Mr Boston being brought from Oxnam, but the Marquess of Lothian, who had the nomination, though the Crown was patron, would not hear of it. On the marquess presenting Mr Boston to Oxnam he promised to give him a better whenever it was in his power, and when Crailing became vacant Mr Boston reminded his lordship of his promise. The marquess informed him that the kirk in question had been promised to a preceptor of the Lothian family long previous to his settlement at Oxnam, but assured him that his promise would be remembered whenever he had the power to fulfil it. Mr Boston, in a letter which showed more bitterness than good taste, replied that his lordship had "acted in this affair neither with the honour of a nobleman nor the faith of a Christian." This was why Lord Lothian would not nominate him for Jedburgh. The great majority of the people of Jedburgh had, however, set their hearts on Mr Boston, who was a popular preacher, and, says a contemporary writer, "Led away by vanity and popular applause, Mr Boston, in opposition to the advice of his best and truest friends, gave up his charge, and threw himself into the arms of the malcontents." These proceedings were the cause of much rancour in the parish (*Autobiography of a Scottish Borderer*).

IN THE SOUTH TRANSEPT.

A little to the west of the foot of the stair leading up to the tower lie the remains of John Ainslie, surveyor, who was born in Jedburgh in 1745, and died in Edinburgh in 1828. His first essay as a draftsman was a plan of the town of Jedburgh on four sheets. In 1775 he surveyed the counties of Kinross and Fife, with the rivers Forth and Tay; and in the following year he offered proposals for an actual survey of the counties of Stirling and Clackmannan, but the undertaking was abandoned. In 1784-85 he surveyed the east coast of Scotland, and published his survey on two large sheets, which was considered a very good performance. His map of Scotland, which was an excellent piece of work, was laid down on nine large sheets. He is said to have been the first who delineated the great valley of Scotland in a straight line from Inverness to Fort-William. He was the author of a much-esteemed treatise on land surveying.

IN THE NAVE.—LORD CAMPBELL.

Lord Campbell and Lady Stratheden, his wife, are interred in a vault in the south aisle of the nave. John Campbell, though descended from a cadet of the ducal house of Argyll, was a son of the manse, his father being minister of Cupar, in Fifeshire. Young Campbell, who was born in 1781, after taking his degree of M.A. at the University of St Andrews, entered himself of Lincoln's Inn, and before being called to the bar in 1806 he acted as reporter and critic for the *Morning Chronicle*. In 1830 he was returned to Parliament for the Borough of Stafford, and four years later he was returned as one of the members for the City of Edinburgh, which city he continued to represent till 1841. He was made Solicitor-General in 1832, when the honour of knighthood was conferred upon him; Attorney-General in 1834; Lord Chancellor of Ireland, with a peerage of the United Kingdom, in 1841; Lord Chief-Justice of England in 1850; and Lord Chancellor of England in 1859. Lord Campbell was author of *The Lives of Lord Chancellors and Keepers of the Great Seal of England, from the Earliest Times till the Reign of George IV.*, and *The Lives of the Chief Justices of England, from the Norman Conquest till the Death of Lord Mansfield*. He died in 1861, after "a fortunate and brilliant career, with an old age of physical and intellectual vigour rarely paralleled." His connection with the district of Jedburgh was as proprietor of the estate of Hartrigge. Lady Stratheden was daughter of Sir James Scarlett, afterwards the first Lord Abinger. She was made Baroness Stratheden in 1836, and died in 1860.

THE CHURCHYARD.

The dead of several centuries lie in the adjoining burying-ground, and yet of all the thousands who have there found a resting-place, comparatively few have left their mark behind them. Generation after generation passeth away and are remembered no more. No one can tell how many "Village Hampdens" and "mute inglorious Miltons" lie there, but there must be not a few of those who took part in the defence of their town during the rude days of Border warfare. It is to many a sacred spot, and to ourselves it has hallowed associations.

Almost close to the north-west gate of the abbey, and on the upper side of the road, is a through-stone to the memory of James Winter, architect, who died in 1790. It bears the following inscription:—" Whoever removes this stone, or causes it to be removed, may he die the last of all his friends." This was no doubt suggested by the well-known lines on Shakespeare's tomb:—

"GOOD FREEND FOR ISVS SAKE FORBEARE,
TO DIGG THE DVST ENCLOASED HEARE;
BLESE BE YE MAN YT SPARES THES STONES,
AND CVRST BE HE YT MOVES MY BONES."

In the *Autobiography of a Scottish Borderer*, James Winter is spoken of as a man of a mind superior to his contemporaries.

A little further down, on the same side of the road, is the grave of Robert Shortreed, who was Sheriff-Substitute for Roxburghshire, and the friend and companion of Sir Walter Scott. To him Sir Walter was indebted for many of his Border stories; and they used to make rides into Liddesdale together in quest of ballads and other material for the works of the then "Great Unknown." Shortreed's opinion was that William Elliot, farmer, Milburnholm, near Hermitage Castle, was the original of Dandie Dinmont; and Lockhart says: "It is certain that the James Davidson, who carried the name of Dandie to his grave with him, whose thoroughbred death-bed scene is told in the Notes to *Guy Mannering*, was first pointed out to Scott by Shortreed himself several years after the novel had established the man's celebrity all over the Border; some accidental report about his terriers and their odd names having alone been turned to account in the original composition of the tale." Shortreed in 1826 gave Sir Walter a ring that had been found in Jedburgh Abbey, which Sir Walter said he would preserve with especial care. Shortreed died in 1829.

Somewhat higher up, a tall obelisk marks the resting-place of Gavin Hilson, M.D., one of the medical staff of the British army in the Peninsular War, and long a practitioner in Jedburgh. He was greatly respected by all, and was a true friend of the poor. He died in 1847.

About a score of yards nearer the churchyard gate is a monument to the memory of Major John Murray, of the 20th Regiment of Foot, who died 21st June 1818, aged thirty-seven years. He was the son of the second daughter of the Hon. George Home, son of Charles, Earl of Home. He commenced his military career in Holland in 1797, shared the dangers and glories of the British armies in Egypt, Italy, Holland, Portugal, Spain, and France; fought in the battles of Maida, Vimiera, Corunna, Vittoria, the Pyrenees, Nivelle, and others, and was wounded in four of these actions. He had the honour of commanding the brave volunteers of the 4th Division at the storming of St Sebastian.

Almost adjoining this is a through-stone to the memory of Margaret Key, mother of Sir David Brewster. Sir David was born in Jedburgh, but was buried in Melrose Churchyard, under the shadow of the abbey.

Close to the iron railing immediately behind the County Buildings is the grave of Alexander Jeffrey, the historian of Roxburghshire. He was bred for the bar, and had, perhaps, a better knowledge of the criminal law of Scotland than any other lawyer in the county. But notwithstanding his arduous professional duties, he found time to cultivate his taste for literature and antiquities, and his crowning effort was *The History and Antiquities of Roxburghshire and Adjacent*

Districts, from the most Remote Period down to the Present Time, in four volumes. He died in 1874.

In the lower part of the churchyard, a little behind the tall monument to Dr Falla, is the tombstone of William Hope of Hopehouse (now Tudhope). He was in many respects a remarkable man. Bred originally to the trade of a blacksmith, he came to Jedburgh, and commenced a foundry in Canongate, in the premises occupied by Mr Fair. He was the first who burned gas in the burgh, having made it for his private use, and he was the first who had a steam-engine in the burgh. He also made great improvements on the printing press, for which he took out a patent, and the Hope Presses were for a long time in great repute. He died in 1847.

Near to this is a plain tombstone of polished Aberdeen granite, which marks the resting-place of the "Beauteous Rosebud" of Burns, Miss Jean Cruickshanks, afterwards Mrs Henderson. In October 1787, while suffering from a cold contracted during one of his journeys, Burns stayed with Mr Cruickshanks, of the High School, Edinburgh. The house was in James' Square, and the poet's time was chiefly occupied in composing songs for the second volume of Johnson's *Museum,* and in hearing Miss Cruickshanks play the melodies on the pianoforte. It was at this time that he composed the song, "A Rosebud in my Early Walk," in which tender reference is made to the young lady who could make such strains on "trembling string or vocal air." He says: "I wrote this song on Miss Jenny Cruickshanks, only daughter to my old friend, Mr William Cruickshanks, of the High School, Edinburgh." In February 1789 Burns again visited Edinburgh, and wrote and inscribed to Miss Cruickshanks the poem beginning with

" Beauteous rosebud, young and gay,
Blooming in the early May."

She became Mrs Henderson on 1st June 1804, and the following announcement appeared in the *Scots Magazine* at the time:—
" *1st June* 1804.—At Jedburgh, James Henderson, writer there, to Miss Jean Cruickshanks, daughter of the deceased William Cruick-

shanks, High School, Edinburgh." The "Beauteous Rosebud" died in the house No. 48 Castlegate, presently occupied by Mr Alfred Hilson, manufacturer.

Immediately behind this is a small tombstone of some interest. It is in memory of Mungo Thomson, who died on 26th September 1735, and bears the following lines:—

> "Here lies a Christian bold and true,
> An antipode to Babel's crew;
> A friend to truth, to vice a terror,
> A lamp of zeal opposing error,
> Who fought the battle of the Lamb,
> Of victory now bears the palm."

Somewhat to the left of this is a tall granite tombstone of neat design, marking the resting-place of, among others, Robert Easton, land surveyor, a devoted and self-taught student of natural science, chiefly astronomy and mathematics, who died in 1823.

Fully more than half-way between this and Winter's tombstone, already mentioned, is that of James Veitch of Inchbonny, optician, self-taught philosopher, astronomer, and mathematician. He enjoyed the friendship of Professor Playfair, Sir Thomas Brisbane, the Earl of Minto, Sir Walter Scott, and other eminent persons. Mr Veitch had the reputation of being one of the best makers of telescopes and philosophical instruments in his day, and the only telescope ever possessed by the celebrated Mary Somerville (who, by the way, was born in the manse of Jedburgh which stood in the abbey garden) was made by him. In the workshop of James Veitch, Sir David Brewster when a boy spent much of his leisure time, and there can be no doubt that these visits to Inchbonny had much to do with the forming of Sir David's tastes for scientific pursuits. Mr Veitch was the first to discover the great comet of 1811, as well as several others; and he contributed a number of articles to the *Edinburgh Encyclopædia*, at the request of Sir David Brewster, who was the editor.

Almost side by side with Mr Veitch lies the Rev. Alexander Shanks, who for nearly forty years was minister of the Associate Congregation in Jedburgh. At Mr Shanks' ordination on 15th

October 1760 the minister who preached on that occasion took for his text, "What will this babbler say?" The question was not left long unanswered. Shanks was a man of considerable talents, and one of his published sermons on "Peace and Order" attracted the attention of the Government of the time, and he was offered a pension. He, however, refused to accept it. "I am loyal from conscience," he said; "a seceder from principle. I have done nothing more than my duty—I take no reward." The stone at the head of his grave was erected in respect for his memory by Blackfriars United Presbyterian Congregation in 1877, the former "frail memorial" having become much decayed.

POSSESSIONS AND REVENUES OF THE ABBEY.

(Abridged from Morton's "Monastic Annals of Teviotdale.")

WE learn from the confirmatory charter of Earl Henry that his father, King David I., when he established the abbot and convent at Jedburgh, made or confirmed to them the following grants of property—the monastery of Jedworthe, with everything belonging to it, namely, the tithes of the two Jedworths, Langton, Nesbyt, and Creling, the town of Earl Gospatric,[1] with the consent of his chaplain; and, in the same town, a ploughgate and a half and three acres of land, with two houses: also the tithes of the other Creling, the town of Orm, the son of Eylav,[2] and of Scrauesburghe: the chapel situated in the forest opposite Hernwingeslawe;[3] also Ulfstoun, near Jedworth; Alneclive, near Alncromb, Crumsethe,[4]

---

[1] Gospatric, one of the sons of Gospatric, Earl of Northumberland, being deprived of his possessions by William the Conqueror, fled into Scotland, where Malcolm III. gave him the territory of Dunbar and other lands in the southern counties. He was the founder of the nunnery of Coldstream. He is styled vice-comes, viscount, or sheriff, in Earl Henry's charter, but in general is simply styled earl. His descendants were the Earls of Dunbar and March, and the present representative is the Earl of Home.

[2] Eilav, or Eilaf, was probably likewise a Saxon baron, who found an asylum in Scotland at the Conquest, and had lands given him by the liberality of the king. Elliestoun, in St Boswells parish, appears to derive its name from him. It was anciently written Ylifstoun. There are several places and many families in Scotland called Ormiston, probably from his son Orm. A family of that name was long settled at Old Melrose.

[3] In King William's charter, Xernwingeslaw. It appears to be the place now called Mervinslaw, on the left bank of the Jed, a little above Old Jedworth.

[4] Crumsethe, otherwise Crumshache and Cromsahie. There is a place called Crumhaugh near Hawick.

and Reperlaw.¹ He also granted them the tenth part of the game taken by him in hunting in Teviotdale; the multure of the miln at Jedworth, where all the people of the town ground their corn; pasture for their cattle in the king's forest, and the right of taking wood and timber for the use of the monastery, except in the place called Quikhege; the village of Rule Hervey,² which he gave them in exchange for a ten pound land in Hardinghestorn;³ and Eadwordisley;⁴ also a salt-work near Striveline;⁵ a house in the town of Roxburg, and another in Berwic; and a fishing in the Tweed, opposite the isle of Tunsmidhop. They obtained afterwards another house in Berwick, with a toft adjacent to it.

Malcolm IV. gave them the churches of Barton and Grendon in Northamptonshire, a toft and seven acres in the town of Jedworth, a fishing above the bridge at Berwick, and exemption from paying duty for their wine imported into that town.

Berengarius de Engain⁶ gave them a merk of silver out of the profits of the miln of Creling, with two oxgangs of land, one villan, or bondservant, and a toft; and, for the maintenance of the chaplain of the same village, he gave two other oxgangs, and two tofts, one of which was beside the church.

David Olifard gave the tithe of the miln of Creling.⁷

Richard English gave two oxgangs of land in Scrauesburghe and two in Langton.

---

¹ Reperlaw is in the parish of Lilliesleaf.
² Now Abbotrule.
³ Probably Hardingstone in Northamptonshire.
⁴ Edwardly, Jedburgh.
⁵ Stirling.
⁶ A noble Anglo-Norman, one of the followers of Earl David, to whom he gave lands in Scotland, after his accession to the throne (Chalmers' *Caledonia*).
⁷ David Olifard was King David's grandson, and much attached to him, although he served in King Stephen's army, which besieged him in Winchester in 1141. When the King of Scots escaped, Olifard concealed him and conducted him to Scotland, for which service he had lands given him in Smailholm and Crailing.

Gamel, who, in King William's charter, is styled "clerk," with consent of his sons, Osulf and Ughtred, gave Caverum.¹

Margaret, the wife of Thomas de London, with consent of her husband, and Henry Lovel, her son, gave Ughtredshaghe.²

Christiana, the wife of Gervas Ridel, gave the third part of the village of Hernwingeslawe.³

Gaufrid de Perci gave the convent, the church of Oxenham, with two ploughgates, and two oxgangs of land adjacent thereto, and right of pasture and fuel in the common; also Newbigging, with common pasture and fuel, as enjoyed by the other inhabitants of the same village.⁴

Ralph, the son of Dunegal, and his wife Bethoc, gave them a ploughgate in Rughechestre, with common pasture.⁵

Turgot de Rossedale gave them the religious house on the Lidal,⁶ with all its adjacent lands; and the church of Kirkhanders,⁷ with everything thereto belonging.

Guido de Rossedale, with the consent of his son Ralph, granted the convent forty-two acres, between the Esk and the Lidal, at the

---

¹ Probably Cavers. There are two places of the name in Teviotdale, distinguished after the names of the proprietors—Cavers Douglas and Cavers Carr.

² The lands of Lessudden were granted to Thomas de London by King David. He married Margaret Lovel, a widow.

³ Gervas Ridel, descended of an Anglo-Norman family of distinction, settled at Ryedale in Yorkshire, came into Scotland with Earl David, and was sheriff of Roxburgh in 1116. The king gave him the lands in the parish of Lilliesleaf, which, though not entailed, continued in the possession of his posterity, by direct male descent, until the twenty-fifth generation.

⁴ Gaufrid, or Geoffrey, de Perci inherited the lands of Heton and Oxenham from his brother Allan, surnamed "le Meschin," who obtained them from King David, for whom he fought at the Battle of the Standard.

⁵ Rule Bethoc, now called Bedrule, was named after this lady. From her descended Randolph, Earl of Moray, the friend of Robert the Bruce. Rughechestre is probably Rewcastle, near Jedburgh.

⁶ This house stood on the site of the priory of Canonby.

⁷ Kirkandrews in Cumberland.

junction of these rivers, with the right of fishing from the foss¹ of Lidal to the church.

Ranulph de Sulas gave them the church of the Vale of Lidal, the church of Dodington near Berton,² and half a ploughgate in Nesbith.

Gervas Lidal [Rydel?], who afterwards became a canon of Jeddeworth, and his brother Ralph, gave them the church of Abboldesle,³ with all its rights and dues.

William de Vetereponte, or Vipont, gave them a ploughgate in his lordship of Caredene,⁴ with common rights.

Waltheof, son of Gospatric, gave them the rectorial church of Bassenthwaite in Cumberland.⁵

The church of Dalmenie in Linlithgowshire was acquired by the convent in the reign of King William or Alexander II. The canons enjoyed the rectorial tithes, and appointed a vicar to serve it. It was valued in 1275 at £2, 13s. 4d.⁶

The church of Hownam in Teviotdale was acquired by the convent about the end of the twelfth century.

King Robert I., among other grants, and confirmation of former grants, to the "priory of Rosinot, and the abbot of Jedworth byding there," confers upon them "the teinds of the king's horses and studs, and the third of the hay of the forest of Platir:" also that they should get, every day that the king remained at Forfar, two loaves of the bread called Sunday bread, four loaves of the second bread, and six of the bread called hagmans; two stoups of the best ale, two

---

¹ Part of this ancient foss, or artificial bank of earth, still exists in a very perfect state on the lands on Liddal-bank, and is called the Railzie.

² Barton in Northamptonshire was the original seat of the Soulis family, who were brought into Scotland by David I. The church of Lidal stood near the junction of the two rivers. It was dedicated to St Martin, and valued in 1275 at £4.

³ Abbotslee in Huntingdonshire.

⁴ Carriden in Linlithgowshire.

⁵ Hutchinson's *History of Cumberland*.

⁶ In Bagimont's Roll.

stoups of the small ale called second ale, and two pair of dishes of each of the three services from the kitchen.[1]

The hospital of St Mary Magdalene at Rutherford was given to the convent in 1377 by Robert III., upon the resignation of Alexander de Symondton, the last master thereof.

There was an altar in the abbey church dedicated to St Ninian, and another to St Mungo.

The property of the monasteries having been confiscated at the reformation of religion, an account of it was taken in 1562, when the revenues of Jedburgh Abbey, together with those of Restenot and Canonby, were estimated at—

£1274, 10s., Scots money; 2 chalders and 2 bolls of wheat; 23 chalders of barley; 36 chalders, 13 bolls, 1 firlot, and 1 peck of meal.

The temporal possessions of the monastery at that time were the baronies of Ulston, Windington, Ancrum, Belses, Reperlaw, and Abbotrule. Its spirituality consisted in the kirks of Jedburgh, Eckford, Hownam, Oxnam, Langnewton, Dalmeny, Selbie, Wauchope, Castleton, Crailing, Nisbet, Plenderleith, and Hobkirk. Of these, Selbie, Wauchope, and Castleton belonged properly to Canonby. To Restenot belonged the kirks of Forfar, Dounyvald, and Aberlemno.

In "Ane Accompt of the Thirds of the Benefices, taken from the Accompts of Robert Lord Boyd, Collector-General of the said Thirds, for the year 1576," are the following articles:—

"Third of the abbacy of Jedburgh, £333, 6s. 8d.; wheat, 11 bolls, 1 firlot, 3 pecks; bear, 7 chalders, 10 bolls, 3 firlots, 2 pecks; meal, 12 chalders, 4 bolls, 1 firlot, 3 pecks; third of the altarage of St Ninian,[2] £3, 4s. 5d."

A new order was issued in 1587 to collect the king's thirds of the benefices, when Jedburgh was to pay £200 and Restenneth £100.[3]

---

[1] Harleian MSS. 4134 and 4693.   [2] Ibid. 4612.   [3] Ibid. 4623, Vol. II.

RENT ROLL OF THE ABBEY.

(From a MS. in the Harleian Collection, No. 4623, Vol. I. Published in "The Monastic Annals of Teviotdale.")

TAXT ROLL OF THE ABBACY OF JEDBURGH, 1626.

"*3rd January 1626.*—In a judicial court of the lordship and abbacy of Jedburgh, holden within the kirk of the said burgh, be Andrew, Master of Jedburgh, baillie principall of the said abbacy, compeared, &c., procurator for the Lord Binning, and produced ane act of convention, holden at Edinburgh, the 27th of Octobir, 1625, where all the vassals fewars were ordained to have conveened that day, with the Lord Binning, for setting down ane taxt roll for his relieffe of the taxation of the saids lordships, with the extension of the said act, with ane certificat under the lord register's hand, anent the taxation of the said lordship, extending at every terme of the four term's taxation, to £516, 13s. 4d.; and upon production thereof, the procurator took infeftment in the hands of the clerk of court. And thereafter the baillie called all the vassals, &c., by name and surname, of the whilks only compeared, &c., after lawful time of day bidden. The next day, being oftentimes called and not compearing, the said procurator protested it might be lawful for him, with the persons before-written compearing, to sett down the said taxt roll, conforme to the warrant granted by the said act of convention; whilk protestation the said baillie admitted; and thereupon the said procurator, with the persons aforementioned, have all with one consent, sett down the said taxt roll, and ordaining, &c. And for the collecting of the said taxation, there shall be augmented yearly, to the said some of 516lib. 13s. 4d., the sowme of 183lib. 6s. 8d.

for inbringing the said taxation. In token whereof, the said baillie and procurator and persons above mentioned sett their hands."

TEMPORAL LANDS OF THE LORDSHIP AND ABBACY OF JEDBURGH.

Rutherford of Handelye, his 10lib. land of Belshes, worth yearly 30 bolls victuall, at 80lib. per chalder; whereof payes to my lord 10lib.

Davidson of Kaymes, for his 5lib. land in Belshes, and 5 merk land in Raperlaw, estimat worth 50 bolls victuall; whereof payes to my lord 8lib. 13s. 4d.

Haliburton of Muirhouselaw, his 10lib. land in Belshes and Pinnacle, worth 64 bolls; payes 11lib.

Turnbull of Wylliespeil, for his merk land of Wylliespeil, estimat to be worth yearly 100lib.; whereof payes 13s. 4d.

Turnbull, for his 3lib. land of Hassenders-bank, estimat to be worth yearly 10 bolls victualls; whereof payes £3.

Sir John Scott of Newburgh, for his 4lib. land of the barony of Belshes, estimat to be worth 24 bolls yearly; payes 4lib.

Scott of Heidshaw, for his £5 in Belshes, estimat to 42 bolls; payes £5.

Sir Robert Ker of Ancrum, for his lands of Ancrum and Woodheid, worth 20 chalder victuall; payes £32.

William Midlemess of Lyllslie Chapell, for £11 of the barony of Belshes, worth 60 bolls vict.; payes £11.

Davidsons in Belshes, for their 4lib. 10sh. land in Belshes, worth 18 bolls vict.; paye £4, 10sh.

Turnbull of ——— for his five merk land of Belshes, worth 30 bolls; payes 5m.

Turnbull, for his £5 land of Abbotrule, worth 10 bolls; payes £5.

Turnbulls, possessors of £12 lands beyond the burn of Abbotrule, worth 24 bolls; paye £12.

Turnbull, for Maksyde, worth yearly 80libs.; payes 5lib.

Turnbulls, for their 42sh. 4d. land of Fodderlye, worth 10 bolls vict.; paye 42sh. 4d.

Thomas Ker, for Gaithuscott, worth 24 bolls; payes 36sh.
Scott of Todrig, for Grange, worth 32 bolls; payes 5 merks.
Foulden, for Netherbourten, worth yearly £100; payes 13sh. 4d.
Turnbull, for Braidhaugh, worth 5 merks: payes 6sh. 8d.
Turnbull, for his lands of Hartishauch, worth 5 bolls; payes 6sh. 8d.
Rutherford, for Woole, worth 10 merks; payes 10sh.
Turnbull, for Overbonchester, worth 6 bolls; payes 30sh.
Turnbull, for his half lands of Eister Swansheill, worth 30lib.; payes 26sh. 8d.
Shiells, for Kirknow and Langraw, 80lib.; payes 5lib.
Kirkton, for the 16 lands of Houston, worth 64 bolls vict.; payes 30lib. 12sh.
Kirkton, for Stewartfield and Chapmansyde, worth 60 bolls; payes 11lib. 4sh.
William Douglas of Bonjedburgh, for his lands of Toftilaw, Padopuill, and Spittlestains, worth 48 bolls vict.; payes £11, 13sh. 4d.
Smart, for his 2 lands in Crailling, worth 8 bolls; payes £22.
Cranston, for Plewlands, and 20sh. land in Nisbitt, worth $34\frac{1}{2}$ bolls; payes 4lib. 6sh. 8d.
Lindores, in Stichell, for his 33sh. 4d. land in Stichell, worth 8 bolls vict.; payes 33sh. 4d.
Hall, for the half of Haugh-heid, worth 15 bolls; payes 33sh. 4d.
The Countess of Bothwell, for the other half, worth 15 bolls; payes 13sh. 4d.
Taitt in Cessford Mayns, for his merk land, yearly worth 2 bolls; payes 13sh. 4d.
Rutherford of Hunthill and Skarsburgh, worth 4 bolls; payes 13sh. 4d.
Ainslie in Oxnam, for his 2 merk land, worth 10 bolls vict.; payes 20sh. 8d.
Robertson in Harden, for his 20sh. land, yearly worth 4 bolls; payes 20sh.
Robertson, for his 20sh. land; payes als much.

Andrew, Master of Jedburgh, for his lands of Newbigging, worth 200 merks; payes 10lib.

Item, for his lands of Auld Jedburgh and Hustneley, worth 14 bolls; payes 20sh.

Tennent, for ane land worth 3 bolls; payes 20sh.

Storie in Rowcastle, for his land, worth 1 boll; payes 5sh.

Porteus, for ane land worth 4 bolls; payes 20sh.

Mader, for 2 lands in Langton, worth 8lib.; payes 40sh.

Earl of Roxburgh, for his 4 merk land of Newhall, worth 100 merks; payes 53sh. 4d.

Eliot of Stobs, for his 25 merk land of Windington,[1] worth 400 merks; payes 25 merks.

Possessors of Hyndhousefield, worth 90 bolls; paye 40 merks.

Possessors of Castlewoodfield, worth 60 bolls; paye 9lib.

Ainslie, for 6 aikers possessed by her, worth 8 bolls: payes 11sh.

Home, possessor of Spittle, worth 8 chalder victuall; free rent.

Gressoun, for his lands in Spittell, worth 1 chalder vict.; payes 5lib.

Ainslie, for his aikers in Boongate, worth 8 bolls vict.; payes 4sh.

Kirkton and Rutherford, for the possessors of the free milns of Jedburgh, worth 4 chald. vict.; paye 90lib.

Earl of Buccleugh, for Cannabie, worth 1200 merks; payes 11lib. 6sh. 8d.

Item, for his lands of Liddisdale, worth 1000 merks; payes 10lib.

Bennet of Chesters, for Raeflatt and Ryknow, worth 2 chald. vict.; payes 8 merks.

Rutherford, for Steepleside, worth 8 bolls; payes 30sh.

Possessors of Sheilfield, worth £40; paye 2sh.

Ker, for Hercass, worth 10 merks; payes 6sh. 8d.

Robeson, for Cruikes, worth 5 merks; payes 6sh. 8d.

Andrew, Master of Jedburgh, for Overwoolismilne, worth 20 bolls vict.; payes 40sh.

Davidson, for Netherwoolis, worth 20 bolls; payes 20sh.

---

[1] Winningtonrig, in Kirktoun parish.

Buckholm, for Belshes milne, worth 24 bolls; payes £20 for money and customs.

Hamilton, for Kinglass, worth 400 merks; payes 6sh. 8d.

Gledstanes, for Cocklaw, worth 1 chald. vict.: payes 20sh.

Turnbull of Bewlie, for 4 aikers in Langnewton, worth 3 bolls; payes 6sh. 8d.

Ker of Ancrum, for Knox and Henfield, worth 100 merks; payes 40sh.

Master of Jedburgh, for Priestfield, worth 10 merks; payes 1 merk.

Trotter, for the Convent Yards, worth 25lib.: free rent.

Ainslie, for his part of the Convent Yards, worth £20; payes 20sh.

Weir, for Seills, worth 500 merks; payes 200 merks.

Ainslie, for the aikers of Boongate, worth £30; payes 10sh.

SPIRITUALITY OF THE ABBEY.

Teynds of Ulstoune, confest to be 24 bolls victuall; whereof payes the minister of Jedburgh 8 bolls.

Teynds of Stewartfield, worth 24 bolls; whereof payes the said minister 16 bolls.

Master of Jedburgh, his teynd sheaves of Woolis, worth 24 bolls; whereof payes the said minister 10 bolls.

The teynd sheaves of Over Crailling, worth 10 bolls; whereof payes to the Earl of Lothian, as lord of erection of the abbacy of Newbattle, 6 bolls.

The teynds of Over Crailling, worth 4 chald. vict.; whereof payes to the Earl of Lothian 2 chalders.

Lord Cranstoun, his teynd sheaves in Nether Crailling, worth 10 chald.; payes said earl 48 merks.

Teynd sheaves of Samiestoun, worth 10 chald.; payes to the minister of Jedburgh 16 bolls.

Teynd sheaves of Renniestoun, worth 4 bolls; payes to the minister of Jedburgh 10 furlots of tack duty.

Teynd sheaves of Hunthill, worth 2 chald.; payes Earl of Lothian 16 bolls.

SPIRITUALITY OF THE ABBEY.

Andrew, Master of Jedburgh, for his whole teynds contened in his tack, worth 10 chald.; payes to the minister of Jedburgh 24 bolls; to the minister of Oxnam 3 chald.; to the minister of Hopkirk 12 bolls; to the Earl of Lothian 3 chald. 8 bolls.

Teynd sheaves of Edgarstoun, worth 2 chald.; payes minister of Jedburgh 1 chald.

Teynds of Auld Jedburgh, worth 12 bolls; paie Earl of Lothian 8 bolls.

William, Earl of Angus, his teynd sheaves of Lintalie, worth 6 bolls; payes to the said earl 4 bolls.

Rutherford, for his teynd sheaves of Swinnie, worth 16 bolls; payes said earl 6lib.

Teynd sheaves of Hundelie, worth 24 bolls; paie minister of Jedburgh 6 bolls.

Teynd sheaves of Castlewood, worth 40 bolls; paid to said earle.

Ker of Ancrum, his teynd sheaves of Jedburghside, worth 40 bolls; payes said earl 12lib.

Teynd sheaves of Gleneslands, worth 16 bolls; paie minister of Jedburgh 14 bolls.

Teynd sheaves of Langtoun, worth 6 chald.

Teynd sheaves of Bonjedburgh, worth 5 chald.; paie said earl 28lib.

Teynd sheaves of Hyndhousefield, worth 40 bolls; paie said earl 20lib.

The Earl of Lothian, for the teynd sheaves of Nisbitts, worth 8 chald. vict.; payes the minister of Crailling 3 chald.

His lordship's teynd sheaves of the Spittel, worth 3 chald.; free rent.

His lordship, for the tack duties before and after specified, paid to him, extends to 25 chald. 3 bolls vict. and £138 of money.

Earl of Buccleuch, for the teynd sheaves of Casseltown, worth 1133lib. 6sh. 8d.; payes to the minister 466lib. 13s. 4d.

Earl of Nithisdaill, for his teynds of Wauchopdaill, worth 400 merks; payes said earl 40 merks.

Countess of Bothwell, for the teynds of Heikfield, Gremishlaw, and Maynes, worth 8 chald.; payes Earl of Lothian 2 chald.

SPIRITUALITY OF THE ABBEY. 157

William Mow of Mowmayns, for the teynd sheaves thereof, worth 2 chalders; free rent.

The said Countess of Bothwell, for the teynd sheaves of Haugh-heid, worth 12 bolls; payes the minister of Jedburgh 8 bolls.

The Earl of Roxburgh, for the teynd sheaves of Cavertoun and Ormistoun, worth 12 chald. vict.: payes to the minister of Eckford 5 chald., and to the Earl of Lothian 3 chald. 12 bolls.

Rutherford, his teynd sheaves of Hownam, worth 10 bolls; payes said earl 4 bolls.

Bessie Ker, Lady Mow, for her part of the teynd sheaves of Hownam, 10 bolls; payes the minister of Hownam 6 bolls.

Pringle of Hownam, his teynd sheaves thereof, worth 10 bolls; payes said minister 4 bolls.

Teynd sheaves of Nether Chatt, worth 8 bolls; paid said Earl of Lothian.

Teynd sheaves of Beirop and Fillogare, worth 10 bolls; paie said earl 5 bolls.

Teynd sheaves of Over Whitsum, worth 10 bolls; paid to the minister of Hownam.

Ker of Chatto, his teynd sheaves of Chatto and Cuishop, worth 20 bolls; payes the minister of Hownam 16 bolls.

Teynd sheaves of Swynsyde, worth 30 bolls; paid to the Earl of Lothian.

Teynd sheaves of Newbigging and Sheills, worth 12 bolls; paye to the Earl of Lothian 8 bolls.

Teynd sheaves of Newtoun, Dolphistoun, and Fala, worth 24 bolls; paie said earl 24 bolls.

Teynd sheaves of Overtoun, worth 16 bolls; paie said earl 12 bolls.

The Earl of Roxburgh, for the teynd sheaves of Plenderleith and Middleknow, worth 8 bolls; payes the Earl of Lothian 20lib.

Stewart of Traquair, for the teynd sheaves of Wollis, worth 10 bolls; payes the minister of Hopkirk 4 bolls.

Turnbull, for his teynd sheaves of Bullerwall, worth 12 bolls; payes to said earl 8 bolls.

Turnbull, for his teynd sheaves of Gledstanes, worth 5 bolls; payes to said earl 2 bolls.

Lord Cranstoun, for the teynd sheaves of Stennalege, Wauchope, Langhauch, and Herwoodtoun, worth 2 chald. vict.; payes the minister of Hopkirk 22 bolls.

Teynd sheaves of Harwood, Applesyde, and half of Hawthornside, worth 17 bolls; paie to said minister of Hopkirk 16 bolls.

Teynd sheaves of Over Halthornside, worth 8 bolls; paye the Earl of Lothian 20lib.

Teynd sheaves of Unthank, worth 1 boll; paid to said earl.

Davidson, for the teynd sheaves of Myre, half-quarter of Belshes, worth 16 bolls; payes said earl 4lib.

Scott of Heidshaw, for the teynd sheaves of the Peill halfe-quarter, worth 24 bolls; payes the said earle 12 bolls.

Teynd sheaves of Pinnacle, worth 16 bolls vict.; paid to said earle.

Teynd sheaves of Ryflatt and Ryknow, worth 8 bolls; paie said earl 4lib.

Cairncross, for the teynd sheaves of the Milnerig quarter of Belshes, worth 12 bolls; payes said earl 10lib.

The few maills and duties particularly afore-mentioned, payed yearly to the said Lord Binning extends to 468lib. 12sh.; whereof payes of blensh duty to the king 380lib.: and payes to Andrew, Master of Jedburgh, hereditary baillie to the said lordship, for his baillie fee, 50lib.; so rests 38lib. 12sh. free rent.

The said Thomas Lord Binning, his teynds of the parochin of Dummenie, worth 20 chald. of victuall; whereof payes to the minister 2 chalders and 400 merks. Rests of free rent, 8lib. per chalder, 1173lib. 6sh. 8d. Taxt to 41lib. 10sh.

CHARTERS RELATIVE TO JEDBURGH ABBEY.

Carta Confirmationis Comitis Henrici[1] Canonicis de Jedworde.

In honorem Sanctæ et individuæ Trinitatis: Ego Henricus comes Northanhumbriorum canonicis patris mei quos in monasterio Sanctæ Mariæ de Jedworde constituit, in perpetuam eleemosinam concedo, et hujus cartæ meæ attestatione confirmo, donatum illis ab eodem patre meo, predictum monasterium de Jedworthe, cum omnibus ad illud pertinentibus, viz., decimas villarum totius parochiæ, sciL duarum Jeddword, et Langton, Nesbyt, Creling, Gospatricii vicecomitis, ipsius Gospatricii capellano ejusdem Creling præfato monasterio concedente, et testibus legitimis confirmante: Et in eadem villa, unam carucatam terræ et dimidiam et tres acras, cum duabus maisuris: Necnon et decimas alterius Creling villæ Orm, filii Eylav; et de Scrauesburghe: Capellum etiam quæ est in saltu nemoris; et decimam totius venationis patris mei in Thevietdale; omnes reditus ad supradictum monasterium juste pertinentes. Preterea villas subscriptas; Ulvestoun juxta Jedworthe, Alneclive juxta Alncromb, Cromseche, Raperlaw, cum rectis divisis ad easdem villas pertinentibus. Unam maisuram in burgo Roxburg, et unam in Berewic, et ibidem unam aquam, liberas, solutas, et quietas. Et Edwordisley, sicut eam pater meus perambulavit et divisas monstravit. Et animalium pascua ubi patris mei. Et ligna silvarum, et materiem ad sua necessaria ubi pater meus, præter illum locum qui vocatur Quikhege. Et multuram molendini Jeddworde, ubi castellum est, de omnibus hominibus

---

[1] Henry, Earl of Huntington and Northumberland, died in 1152, the year preceding the death of his father, King David.

ejusdem Jeddworde. Et unam salinam juxta Strevelin. Volo itaque et concedo ut omnia quæcumque modo possident aut deinceps juste possessuri sint, ita libere et pure, omni remota exactione, supradicti canonici patris mei cum omnibus monasterii sui libertatibus et liberis consuetudinibus pace perpetua possideant, sicut illis pater meus eadem beneficia, carta et auctoritate sua, possidenda precepit et confirmavit. Testibus presentibus: Herb. Glasg. Episcopo: Arnaldo, Abbate de Calco; Eng. cancellario; Adam, capellano: Hugone de Morcvilla; Thoma de Londoniis; Ranu. de Sola, &c.

Charter by King William the Lion to the Canons of Jedburgh in 1165.

(Original in possession of the Duke of Buccleuch. A facsimile is published in the "National MSS. of Scotland," Part I.).

Williemus Dei gratia rex Scottorum, episcopis, abbatibus, prioribus, comitibus, baronibus, justiciariis, vicecomitibus, cæterisque hominibus totius terræ suæ, Francis, Anglis, et Scottis, cunctisque sanctæ Dei ecclesiæ filiis salutem. Ex suscepto regimine regni incumbit nobis ecclesiam Dei et ecclesiasticos diligere personas, et non solum de nostris eis benefacere, sed et beneficia ab aliis Dei fidelibus eis collata auctoritate regia confirmare, et cum sua eis integritate conservare. Inde est quod nos, consilio proborum hominum nostrorum, possessiones et bona quæ, a predecessoribus nostris et ab aliis regni nostri principibus et fidelibus, Deo et ecclesiæ Sanctæ Mariæ de Jeddeworth et canonicis ibidem Deo servientibus collata sunt, præsenti eis privilegio confirmamus: Videlicet, ex dono regis David monasterium de Jeddeworth cum omnibus ad illud pertinentibus; capellam quoque quæ fundata est in saltu nemoris contra Xernwingeslawe; decimam totius venationis regis in Thevietdale, Ulvestonam, Alneclive, juxta Alnecrumb, Crumesethe, Raperlawe, cum rectis divisis ad eas villas pertinentibus, in bosco et plano, pratis, pascuis, et culturis; unam maisuram in burgo Rochesburg; unam maisuram in Berewico; tertiam quoque maisuram in eodem Berewico super Tuedam, cum tofto suo circumjacente; unam aquam quæ est contra insulam quæ vocatur Tonsmidhop; Eadwardesle; pascua animalium proprie, ubi et regis; ligna nemoris, et materiem ad suas necessitates ubi et ipse, præter in Quikeheg: molturam molendini de omnibus hominibus Jeddeworth ubi castellum est; unam salinam juxta Strevelin: Rulam Herevei per suas rectas divisis in nemore et plano, pratis, et pascuis, et aquis, et in omnibus rebus ad eandem villam juste pertinentibus, datam in escambio decem libratarum terræ quas præfati canonici habuerant in Hardinghestorn: ex dono dilecti fratris mei regis Malcolmi, ecclesiam de Bartona, et ecclesiam de Grendona; et in burgo meo de Jeddeworth unum toftum et septem acras; et in domibus suis quas habent in burgo meo de Berewico talem libertatem, scilicet, ut nullus ministrorum regis tunella vini a mercatoribus illic allata et ibi evacuata exigere præsumat; et unam piscariam in Tuede, illam, scilicet, quæ est supra pontem, quam Willielmus de Lambertona avo meo liberam et quietam reddidit; ex dono Gospatricii vicecomitis, in Craaling unam carrucatam terræ et dimidiam, et tres acras, cum duabus maisuras; ex dono Berengarii Engain, unam marcam argenti in molendino ejusdem Craaling, et duas bovatas terræ cum uno villano et uno tofto; et ad sustentamentum victus capellani capellæ ejusdem villæ servituri alias duas bovatas terræ cum alio tofto et unum aliud toftum juxta ecclesiam; ex dono David Olifard decimam molendini ejusdem Craaling; ex dono Oromi filii Eilavi, unam carrucatam terræ in altera Craaling; ex dono Ricardi Angli duas bovatas terræ in Scrauesburg, et duas bovatas terrae in Langetun; ex dono Gameli, clerici, Caverum, Osulfo et Ughtredo filiis ejus concedentibus illius donationem; ex dono Margaritæ, uxoris Thomæ de London, concedentibus eodem Thoma et Henrico Lovel filio ejusdem Margaritæ, Ughtredesxaghe cum suis rectis divisis; ex dono Christianæ, uxoris Gervasii Ridel, tertiam partem villæ de Xernwingeslawe; ex dono Gaufridi de Perci, ecclesiam de Oxenham, cum duabus carrucatis terræ et duabus bovatis eidem ecclesiæ adjacentibus, et communem pasturam et communem foaliam ejusdem Oxenham et Niwebigginghe et communem pasturam et communem foaliam cum cæteris hominibus ejusdem villæ de Oxenham, quam,

L

scilicet, Niwebigging, Henricus de Perci post mortem prædicti G. fratris sui, ante dilectum fratrem meum regem Malcolmum, concessit canonicis datam; ex dono Rod. filii Duneg. et uxoris ejus Bethoc, unam carrucatam terræ in Rughechestre, et communem ejusdem villæ pasturam; ex dono Turg. de Rossedale, domum religionis de Lidel, cum tota terra ei adjacente; ecclesiam quoque de Kirchanders, cum omnibus ad illam pertinentibus; ex dono Guid. de Rossedale, assensu et consensu Rad. filii sui, quadraginta duas acras inter Esch et Lidel, ubi Esck et Lidel conveniunt, et libertatem aquæ a fossa de Lidel usque ad ecclesiam de Lidel; ex dono Ran. de Sol. ecclesiam de valle Lidel, et ecclesiam de Dodinton, juxta Bertonam, et dimidiam carrucatam terræ in Nasebith; ex dono Ger. Ridel, qui post factus est canonicus Jeddeworth, et Rad. fratris sui, ecclesiam de Alboldesle, cum omnibus pertinentibus et rectitudinibus suis; ex dono Willielmi de Veteriponte, unam carrucatam terræ de dominio suo in Caredene cum communi aisiamento villæ. Hæc autem omnia, ita integre et plenarie, Deo, et Beatæ Mariæ, et supradictis canonicis, concedo et confirmo, sicut in autenticis prædecessorum meorum et aliorum proborum virorum, qui bona prædicta eis contulerunt, scriptis continetur. Volo, itaque, ac firmiter præcipio, ut omnia quæcunque modo possident, vel deinceps juste possessuri sint, ita libere et pure, omni remota exactione, suprafati canonici mei, pace perpetua, cum omnibus monasterii sui libertatibus liberisque consuetudinibus, confirmatione et auctoritate mea possideant, sicut aliqui canonici possessiones et libertates liberasque consuetudines sui monasterii, sive quælibet ecclesiastica jura, liberus, quietius, atque honestius possident. Hujus autem concessionis et confirmationis meæ testes hi sunt: Ric. episcopus de Sancto Andrea; Eng. episcopus de Glasg. Joh. abbas de Calceo; Ever. abbas de Holmcultr. Nich. cancellarius; Matth. archid. de Sto. Andr. Ric. capellanus; Walterus fil. Alni; Ric. de Moreville; Phil. de Valoniis; Rob. Avenel; Bernardus fil. Brien; Gilleb. fil. Richerii; David Ovieth. ap. Pebles.

(From "Great Seal Register," Vol. II.).

Apud Edinburgh, 14 July 1511.—Rex dedit extractum de registro carte Roberti (L) regis, sub manu M. Gawini Dunbar archidiaconi S. Andree, rotulorum, &c., clerici [qua Rex Robertus divine caritatis intuitu confirmavit et innovavit abbati et conventui de Jedburgh, priori et canonicis ejusdem loci apud Rostinot commorantibus et ibidem Deo servientibus et hospitalitatem tenentibus, et eorum successoribus, terram de Rostinot super quam ecclesia de R. fundata est. Dunynad, Dissarth, Cragnathrane, Petrechin, Eglispedris, Ardworkis, unum toftum in villa de Perth, unum toftum in villa de Forfare, et unum toftum in villa de Montrose; item annum redditum 20 solidorum 10 denariorum de thanagio de Thanatus, secundas decimas thanagiorum de Veteri Montrose, Duny, Glammys, Kingalteny, et Aberleminoch; item tria bondagia de Forfare, scilicet, Trebogis, Walmerschenour, et Ester-Forfare, et decimam ville de Montrose, molendini et piscarie ejusdem, &c., ann. red. 2 mercarum de villa de Forfare, et 1 merc, de molendino ejusdem, 100 anguillarum de lacu ejusdem, 6 merc. de baronia de Ketnes, 40 sol. et unam peciam terre de baronia de Brechin; unam peciam terre et 1 merc. de parvo Perth, 4 merc. de Inverlunane; integram decimam lucrorum, finium et eschætarium tam curie justiciarie quam vicecomitatus infra vic. Forfare; item decimam wardarum et reieviorum ibidem contingen., decimam equitii domus regis in vic. de Forfare, et decimam feui foreste de le Platan; item in quolibet adventu regis apud Forfare quolibet die 2 panes, de dominico 4 panes, de secundo pane, et 6 panes qui dicuntur *hugmans*, 2 laginas de meliore cervisia, et 2 laginas de secunda cervisia, et 2 paria ferculorum de quolibet trium cursuum de coquina; item decimam percipere de predictis terris regis dominicis in manu regis retentis, perinde ac si in assedatione essent; in quibus fuerunt infeodati per predecessores regis, et quarum in possessione fuerunt tempore Alexandri (III.) regis ultimo defuncti, sicut constabat per inquisitionem ad capellum regis retornatam per fideles homines patrie de Angus; et carte et munimenta dict. religiosorum per guerras et alios casus fortuitos perdita sunt et distructa.—Apud Dunde 1 Mar. an. reg. 16 (1321–22)].

(FROM "GREAT SEAL REGISTER," VOL. IV.).

Apud Edinburgh, 6 July 1566.—Rex et Regina confirmaverunt cartam factam per And. commendatarium perpetuum de Jedburgh, et ejusdem conventum [qua pro ingentibus pecuniarum summis ad reparationem monasterii sui per Anglos combusti, ac pro præsidio et auxilio contra ecclesie hostes et alios quoscunque impensis et impendendis, ad feudifirmam dimiserunt (quondam) Domine Mariote Haliburtoun uni trium heredum domini de Dialtoun, heredibus ejus et assignatis; terras et villam de Ulstoun, Ovir Mains de U., terras de Greithillis, Priourmedois, Chepmansyde, cum earum silva, Spittelstanis, 3 terras husbandias in Craling-Nethir, dimidiam ter. husb. in Ovir Nysbet, 1 ter. husb. in Nethir Nysbet, terras de Plewlandis, terras de Sinlawis vocatas Newhall, terras de Haucheid, terram in Cesfurdburne, terras de Justiceley cum earum decimis, terras de Auld Jedburgh, Rowcastell, peciam terre in Langnewtoun, terras et villam de Abbotisroule, terras de Bowatsyde, Grange, cum molendino Fodderlie, Ovir et Nethir Bunchestir, cum silvis earundem, terras de Maxsyde, Gaithouscat cum silvis, Hartishauch, terras de Langraw cum decimis, terras et villam de Raperlaw, terras de Fyrth cum earum decimis et silvis, terras de West-Bernis cum decimis, terras vocat. Brewlandis in Raperlaw, terras de Belches cum molendino, terras et villam de Ovir Ancrum cum molendino et cottagiis, terras de Hynehousfield (exceptis 15 acris M. Roberto Richertsoun thesaurio regine assedatis) Castelwode et Castelhill cum silvis, cum acris jacen. apud locum Fratrum Minorum de Jedburgh (exceptis 40 solidat. de Castelwode per M. Joh. Rutherfurde et ejus tenentes occupatis, et 40 solidat. vocat. Litle Eschauch olim occupatis per quond. M. Pat. Achesoun et tunc per dictum M. Joh. R.), ac terras dominicales de Spittell vocat. Ancrum-spittell et manerium earumdem, cum molendinis et decimis, vic. Roxburgh; et ordinaverunt dictum manerium de Ancrum fore principale messuagium omnium dict. terrarum. Solvend. dicto monast. 230 lib. 13 sol. 4 den. pro antiquis firmis, gressumis, pultreis, devoriis, ariagiis, cariagiis, canis, &c., et 9 marc. in augmentationem rentalis; necnon duplicando feudifirmam in introitu heredum; ac prestando tres sectas ad tria placita capitalia apud dictum monasterium; cum precepto sasine directo Willelmo Myllare.—Apud dictum monast. 18 Mar. 1559.]

Necnon aliam cartam dictorum Andree, &c. [qua pro pecuniarum summis sibi persolutis, aliisque gratitudinibus, &c., ad feudifirmam dimiserunt dicte Mariote, relicte Georgii Domini Home, heredibus ejus et assignatis, tenementum terre infra burgum de Jedburgh ex parte australi vici regii (inter tenementum quond. Jacobi Reddale tunc Roberti Rutherfurde, aquam de Jedburgh et *lic Abbayclois*) in baronia de Ulstoun, vic. Roxburgh. Solvend. annuatim dicto monast. 4 lib. et duplicando, &c.—Apud dictum monast. 19 Maii 1562.]

THE ABBEYS OF TEVIOTDALE

AS SHOWING

THE DEVELOPMENT OF GOTHIC ARCHITECTURE.

THE ABBEYS OF TEVIOTDALE, AS SHOWING THE DEVELOPMENT OF GOTHIC ARCHITECTURE.

THE abbeys of Teviotdale form a very remarkable group of ruins. They were all founded during the first half of the twelfth century, within a radius of ten miles, and in a district inhabited by a rude and warlike race. The wisdom that prompted their erection can no more be doubted than the pious motives that led to their endowment. Previous to the above date there had existed in the district three religious houses of some note—namely, one at Dryburgh, which had its origin in the sixth century under St Moden; one at Old Melrose, founded in the seventh century by the saintly Aiden; and the other at Geddewrd (Jedburgh), founded two centuries later by Bishop Ecgred of Lindisfarne. These were, however, but glimmering lights, ill fitted to illume the social darkness, as compared with the splendid establishments that afterwards arose.

About the year 1118, David, the "sair saunct," founded a monastery for Canons Regular of the Order of St Augustine, near to the royal castle on the Jed. Shortly afterwards a similar establishment was founded at Kelso for Tironensian monks, one at Melrose for Cistercians, and another at Dryburgh for canons of the Premonstratensian Order. The Churchmen at that time, in addition to being the disseminators of religious principles, were the only persons who were skilled in the peaceful arts and sciences, so that they might well be called the leaders in civilisation. For a century and a half all went well with them. The convent bell rung for matin and vesper services in tranquil security; pious people showered gifts on the already rich ecclesiastics, and kings and nobles were regaled with princely magnificence in the great halls of the monasteries. But a change came. During the disastrous wars between England and Scotland sad havoc was made on those places, hitherto held sacred. The abbeys were cast down or committed to the flames by the English soldiery, and it is owing, in no small degree, to the restorations thus rendered necessary that they are now so interesting to the architect and antiquary. The student of Gothic architecture will find in this very limited district all the essentials for a somewhat minute knowledge of the art in all the stages of its development. Distance may, and often does, "lend enchantment to the view;" but we feel sure that the Scottish student will travel far without finding better examples than those to be met with here. Though it is, of course, the professional architect who alone will be able fully to appreciate the intricacies of mouldings and other minutiæ, there is much in the general character of the different styles that may be studied with advantage by others. After the Reformation, Gothic architecture became entirely neglected in Scotland; but within recent years things have greatly changed for the better in this respect. Not only in the cities, but also in rural parishes, many Gothic structures, not unworthy to be compared with some of the olden time, have been erected within the last quarter of a century; while every year sees the stream of visitors to the old abbeys increasing. The purpose of the following notes, which are necessarily more of a suggestive than of an exhaustive character, is to point out the development of Gothic architecture in the abbeys of Teviotdale.

Gothic architecture is generally divided into three periods or styles, each having its own distinctive features; but as these gradually pass into each other, it is sometimes difficult to determine where one ends and the other begins. The Norman, which was a subdivision of the Romanesque—just as the latter was a modification of Roman architecture—is now held to have been the parent of the Gothic or Pointed styles. In many of the ecclesiastical ruins throughout the country the transition is very marked, and nowhere more so than in the abbeys under notice.

In the choir and some adjoining parts in Jedburgh Abbey there is Norman work dating, it is believed, from the period of the foundation. Many changes have taken place in the older portions, but the original work can be easily distinguished by its heavy round pillars and semicircular arches. There was very little ornamentation on early Norman work, the mouldings being few and simple. We have no windows nor doorways belonging to this early period. The former were very small and plain, while the latter were generally decorated round the arch. Each of the original arches here are of three orders. The lowest are semicircular, while the others, which recede behind, present a stilted appearance, their spring being somewhat higher up. Most of the arches are square-edged; in some the square edge has given place to the bowtell moulding, while others are further decorated with the zigzag ornament; and in the subdividing arches in the triforium on the south side the voussoirs are rounded. Those on the north side are a later insertion. The peculiar arrangement of the arches in the basement storey is worth noting. They spring from corbels inserted in the sides of the pillars, instead of rising from capitals. The bases of the pillars are plain, with a small chamfer at the upper edge, and the capitals are either cushion-shaped or simply notched down towards the neck mould. The abacus is square, with a hollow chamfer at the upper edge, and some of the hood-moulds and string-courses are similar in character. The other mouldings are mostly round with shallow hollows.

On coming to the Transition Norman period, three of the four abbeys have to be noticed—namely, Kelso, Dryburgh, and Jedburgh. Kelso is wholly of Transition Norman character; and from the general massiveness of the structure it has been said to resemble a Norman castle more than a religious edifice. Like the other abbeys it is cruciform, but differs from them in respect that the head of the cross is towards the west instead of towards the east. The transepts and three sides of the tower, a few pillars and arches on the south side of the eastern limb, and a portion of the western part are all that now remain of what was one of the wealthiest abbeys in Scotland. The transepts, as also the west end, are only two bays in length; but there is nothing to show how far the building extended eastward. This abbey was founded in 1128—ten years after Jedburgh—and from the style of the architecture we are inclined to think that its erection would begin almost immediately after the completion of the early Norman work above described. Several new features are introduced here. The pillars of the lower storey are short and round, with additional members to support the sub-arches, which, however, have disappeared. The great piers of the tower are composed of a number of members in a clustered form, many of them comparatively light, and these piers support pointed arches, each of three orders, with chamfered edges. They are the only pointed arches in the building, with the exception of some near the top of the tower. The other arches are all semicircular, some square-edged, and others moulded. The capitals are varied in character; many of them are simply notched, some foliated, and others enriched with different kinds of ornamentation. The abaci are invariably square, but not always plain. Most of the capitals in the upper storeys project exceptionally far from the neck-mould of the shafts—a feature more noticeable here than perhaps in any other building in the country. The pointed bowtell moulding, which appeared about the same time that the pointed arch came into general use, is prevalent here, along with the earlier round bowtell; while in the arch of the north doorway the bowtell is seen with a hollow or groove in it. In addition to the earliest form of string-course, as seen in Jedburgh, there are examples decorated with the zigzag ornament. In the two doorways the ornamentation is profuse. That in the north transept shows, besides the more common mouldings, the star, the nail-head, and the single billet; and the label-mould is composed of a series of circles linked together. Over this doorway is an interlaced arcade, surmounted by a pediment, the face of which is crossed by mouldings forming a kind of lozenge-shaped diaper work. The west doorway, of which only one side now remains, has representations of the bone, the cable, the chevron of different kinds, the beak-head, &c. The windows are long, narrow, and undivided, the only exceptions being two of circular form near the top of the transept gables (that in the south all but gone), an ornamented quatrefoil (only half of which remains) near the top of the west gable, and other quatrefoils of smaller size and plainer form in the upper part of the tower. The interior is greatly lightened by the open arcades which run along the upper storeys; and the interlaced attached arcade on the lower storey of the transepts and western part also forms a very pleasing feature. In the end wall of the south transept is a piscina, a small basin in a niche, in which the officiating priest would wash his hands and the chalice at the celebration of mass, and near to which there would be an altar in former times. The nave, chancel, and transepts seem to have been roofed with wood, while the side aisles were covered with stone, as in Jedburgh, the groin ribs being pointed. A small cell, possibly the sacristy, to the south of the west doorway of the church, has a stone roof of barrel vaulting.

Turning to Dryburgh, the visitor will be pleased to find that the enterprise of modern times has not yet dared to encroach on its peaceful seclusion. Instead of being, like some of the other abbeys, surrounded with buildings out of all sympathy with such relics of the past, Dryburgh is beautifully situated amid grand old trees and verdant fields. The Austin canons frequently chose to have their houses erected near to towns, as at Jedburgh, while the Cistercians and Premonstratensians preferred a secluded spot, as at Melrose and Dryburgh. One is sorry to find here comparatively little of the church remaining, but the feeling of regret is greatly lessened by the fact that considerable portions of the conventual buildings still exist, and that the cloister court is all but entire. With the exception of a few later additions and alterations, these, as also St Moden's chapel—a small apartment at the north-east corner of the cloister court—belong to the Transition Norman. The architecture of the eastern elevations—heavy and severe—points unmistakably to about the middle of the twelfth century. The mullioned windows, with transoms, in what is called the abbot's parlour, are, of course, the work of later hands, and must not be taken into account. The chapter-house windows, looking eastward, are pointed; a pointed oval-shaped light is seen in St Moden's chapel, and all the others in the original work have semicircular arches, like the doorways. The walls in several places are pierced with small openings, called bullet windows. Pilaster-like buttresses support the walls, and the mouldings are of the earliest forms. In St Moden's chapel there seems to have been an altar, as there is a piscina in one of the side walls, and on the floor immediately below is a stone basin, ornamented near the edge with the nail-head, and having a drain passing into the ground. Inside the chapter-house are the remains of interlaced arcading, and it will be observed that the abaci here are circular instead of being square, like those we have previously seen. Over this spacious apartment, fifty feet long by twenty broad, is a cylindrical or barrel-vaulted roof of stone, and the other existing roofs of the same period are of similar character. The abbot's parlour, the library, and refectory are roofless; but we are thankful that these places, so associated with the domestic life of the monks, should have been even partially preserved from the ravages of time, and the still more cruel hands of man. Several vaulted passages run through the buildings, and under the refectory, which occupied the whole south side of the cloister court, are the almonry and wine cellars. Towards the back of the north-west corner of the cloisters are three dungeons, in which, it is said, the disobedient were kept and punished. In one of them, a hole, large enough to admit a man's hand, has been cut in the wall, into which the refractory prisoners' hands were thrust and fastened with a wedge. The hole is placed low enough to allow any one so circumstanced to kneel, but not to sit or lie down. The only light admitted into this gloomy place of confinement was by an opening two inches wide.[1] The cloisters were dedicated in September 1208—fifty-six

---

[1] It was in one of these miserable dungeons that the unfortunate female wanderer mentioned by Sir Walter Scott, in a note to the *Eve of St John*, in the *Minstrelsy of the Scottish Border*, took up her abode, and which she never quitted during the day. When night fell she issued from her habitation, and went to the house of Mr Haliburton of Newmains, or to that of Mr Erskine of Shieldfield, two gentlemen of the neighbourhood, from whom she received charity. "At twelve each night," says Scott, "she lighted her candle, and returned

years after the arrival of the monks—and hence we are prepared to find in them work of a more advanced character than that already alluded to. The doorways in the south-east and north-east corners of the cloister court, and that at the west end of the chapter-house, are good specimens of late Transition. They are all round-headed, with boldly-cut pointed bowtell mouldings and deep hollows, nook-shafts, and foliated capitals. In the last-named doorway the mouldings of the innermost order rise from the base and run round the arch without a break. This order consists of the pointed bowtell, with pretty well-developed dog-tooth ornaments in the side hollows. The abaci in these doorways are square. At each side of the chapter-house doorway just mentioned is a short two-light window of similar character, each being subdivided by a round shaft. It is probable that the interlaced arcade inside may be of the same date.

The nave of Jedburgh Abbey may, without hesitation, be pronounced to be unrivalled as a specimen of Transition Norman. Grand in conception, exquisite in execution, and simple in detail, it is a perfect "thing of beauty." It measures 130 feet in length, consists of nine bays, and is three storeys in height. Instead of round massive piers, as in the choir, we have here graceful clustered pillars. Most of the arches are of a light and pointed character; the archivolts are all moulded, and while the pointed bowtell has been adopted in the lower and middle storeys, where the capitals are foliated and the abaci square, the round bowtell is retained in the clerestory, where the capitals are plainer and the abaci have lost their square edges. There is one example in the triforium where the abacus

---

to her vault, assuring her friendly neighbours that during her absence her habitation was arranged by a spirit, to whom she gave the uncouth name of 'Fat Lips,' describing him as a little man, wearing iron shoes, with which he trampled the clay floor of the vault to dispel the damps. The cause of her adopting this extraordinary mode of life she would never explain. It was, however, believed to have been occasioned by a vow that, during the absence of her lover, she would never look upon the light of day. He never returned, as he fell during the Civil War of 1745-46, and she never more beheld the light of day."

shows a series of rounds, and this form has been adopted in the cloister doorway on the south side. Over each of the lower arches there are in the triforium two pointed arches (included in one of a semicircular form), and four in the clerestory, while the corbel-course at the wall-head is so arranged as to form eight miniature arches within the like space. The subsidiary arches in the triforium are supported on slender shafts, which give a lightness to this part, not surpassed even in the later styles; and the arches in the clerestory, every alternate two of which are pierced for windows, are so light as to have the appearance of supporting themselves without pressure on those under them. The cloister doorway, which has the round arch, is of very delicate design, and consists of four orders. The carving represents human figures, animals of different kinds—some of them of a nondescript character—birds, the chevron ornament, and abundance of foliage, both leaves and branchlets. The great western doorway, also semicircular in the arch, is more deeply recessed, and in addition to a somewhat similar ornamentation, it has the fish-bone, the chain, the star, small dog-tooth, and the nail-head. Both doorways had originally jamb shafts, which are now gone. Some years ago a facsimile of the cloister doorway was made from drawings by Dr R. Rowand Anderson, Edinburgh, under instructions from the Marquess of Lothian, the proprietor. The new doorway was erected in the same wall as the old one. Over the western doorway are three niches with trefoil arches, and above these is a large one-light round-headed window 18 feet 10 inches in height by 5 feet 8 inches in breadth. At each side of this has been an attached arcade with banded shafts and pointed arches, but most of the shafts have disappeared. The St Catherine's wheel window at the top of the gable is of later date. The Norman architects paid considerable attention to the decoration of flat surfaces, as they had but few mouldings at their command, but this was in a great measure discontinued when mouldings became more diversified. It has been pointed out by authorities that one law pervades all the Norman mouldings, and that "they are invariably arranged on rectangular faces, so that two lines at right angles would exactly touch the front face and under portion of the moulding." Two mouldings, both string-courses, are worth pointing out as an advance on those we have already mentioned. One of them, consisting of a hollow, with round members at the side, crosses the west gable immediately above the doorway; and the same kind of moulding is also seen above the centre window. The other, which consists of a chamfer, a fillet, and a pointed bowtell, runs under the lower windows, and had been continued along the north aisle wall. This wall, which had been all but wholly removed, has been partially restored, with portions of the pilaster-like buttresses to show the original design. Two of the original buttresses are yet seen at the north-west corner. The north aisle had been lighted by round-headed one-light windows similar to those at the west end, and the south aisle was lighted by windows rising from the wall head. The side aisles were vaulted with stone in a similar way as the choir chapels already referred to, but the mouldings of the intersecting ribs were pointed. We may mention that in this abbey, as in many other Roman Catholic churches, the north aisle is a foot wider than the south aisle, this being, it is said, to commemorate a tradition to the effect that when the Saviour died on the Cross His head fell towards the right shoulder.

The pointed part of the chancel would appear to have been built shortly after the nave, as it is a nearer approach to Early English. Windows of the earlier period were but small, and when coloured glass came into general use in churches it was found necessary to have them larger, so as to admit sufficient light to the interior. To carry out the design of enlarging the chancel both in height and length, the Early Norman apse and clerestory had to be taken down, and on erecting the newer work some new features were introduced. Here we observe the stilted arch for the first time, and in none of the other abbeys is it to be seen. These arches are called "stilted" because the springings of the arches are above the levels of the imposts, and the mouldings are continued perpendicularly down to the capitals. The clerestory, only part of which remains, consists of a detached arcade, each alternate arch being larger than the others for the insertion of windows. Under this, to the east of the side chapels, was another arcade of a similar kind, but the arches and lights were much larger; and, again, under this was an attached arcade. This part of the building is, unfortunately, much dilapidated, but sufficient remains to show a very beautiful arrangement. The buttresses project considerably further from the face of the wall than those of the nave. The windows are lancet-shaped, and the outer mouldings rise from the bottom of the jambs, and take the arch without a break. The capitals, however, of the inside arcades still cling to the earlier form, and the square abacus is held by Ricman to be the best mark of Transition Norman.

It has been already stated that Kelso Abbey is wholly of Transition Norman character. The Early English is, however, represented by a small doorway, which was rebuilt a number of years ago with stones found in the abbey ruins, and now forms the entrance to the abbey house garden close by. It has a very fine trefoil arch. The capitals are bell-shaped, and the principal mouldings are the roll and fillet, with deep hollows, in which are good specimens of the dog-tooth ornament. This is in the form of a four-leaved flower, projecting in the centre, and is believed to be so named from its fancied resemblance to the dog-toothed violet. In the fully-developed specimens there are perforations under the leaves. There is nothing of a later period.

The greater portion of the abbey church of Dryburgh has been of this style, but, as previously stated, little of it has been preserved. St Mary's aisle and the aisle beyond, forming the north transept, are the most perfect portions. The under pillars are clustered, and support pointed arches of three orders, the sub-arches being chamfered and the outer ones moulded. The groined stone roofs are intersected with more ribs than any we have yet met with in our survey, showing the gradual advance that was being made at that time. The windows in the lower storey are lancet-shaped, and decorated with the dog-tooth. The triforium is lighted by cusped circles of no great dimensions, one of these—a quatrefoil—having the cusps open at the points and turned to both sides. The clerestory is an open arcade of pointed arches, all moulded, some of which are trefoil, and the arches are larger where the wall behind is pierced with windows. The buttresses also show a greater degree of development, in respect that they project further at the base, and recede in stages towards the wall-head. But a more decided advance is seen in the large window of the south transept gable, which is divided by four mullions, forming five lancet-shaped lights, under one principal arch. It has, however, no tracery. Of the chancel only the lower part of the walls remains, and the nave, with the exception of the west gable, has almost wholly disappeared.

The west doorway, because of its semicircular arch, has by some writers been erroneously called Norman, but in reality it belongs to the Decorated period. The form of the arch alone determines nothing as to its date, as the round arch was never totally abandoned in Scotland. The accessories must also be taken into consideration. This doorway consists of three orders, with no jamb shafts. From moulded bases of several members the roll and fillet mouldings rise and pass unbroken round the arch, and in broad hollows between them are rows of square four-leaved flowers. It is altogether unlike work of the earlier period. The St Catherine's wheel in the west gable of the refectory and the alterations in the abbot's parlour may have been executed about the same time.

In Jedburgh there is a greater variety of decorated work. The north transept with its shelving buttresses—in the face of one of which is a finely ornamented niche—and its traceried windows is a fair specimen. The two west windows are simply chamfered at the sides, and each is divided by one mullion, also chamfered, with trefoils and a quatrefoil at the top; but the great north window has at the jambs numerous round and hollow mouldings somewhat flattened, which pass right up to the top of the arch. It is divided by three mullions, also moulded, and the whole of the inside of the arch is filled with flowing tracery. These windows, as well as all others afterwards to be noticed, are pointed. There is a very fine and bold roll and fillet moulding inside the transept, under the north window.

The greater part of the small chapel on the south side of the choir is of the same style, though probably a little later. Here we have a window with two moulded mullions. The principal features of tracery consist of a large quatrefoil with cusps perforated at the surrounding circle, and two pear-shaped lights. There are two corbels in the wall—one representing a human figure as if crushed down by bearing the weight of the groin, and the other a cluster of foliage tied underneath. From these spring ribs with hollow mouldings, which meet at the bosses the round ribs of the Norman period. The chapel wall is supported by two shelving buttresses—one placed at right angles, with a shield bearing the arms of Bishop Turnbull of Glasgow, and the other placed diagonally, a position frequently adopted in the later styles, where buttresses were required at the quoins. The tower is more massive than ornamental, and possesses less architectural beauty than any other portion of the fabric. It is pierced towards the top with several narrow openings with cusped trefoil heads, some of which are windows, while those on the north and south sides are so formed as to allow the emission of sound, the upper storey having evidently been erected for a peal of bells. At the wall-head, immediately under the balustrade (which, by the way, is modern), are several grotesque representations of human heads, some of the faces showing considerable contortion in consequence of the mouths being pulled apart by fingers inserted at the sides. The St Catherine's wheel at the top of the west gable, similar to that at Dryburgh, also belongs to the Decorated period. It has been supposed that the circle in the centre of the wheel was meant to represent the Saviour, and that the twelve spokes which radiate from the centre were emblematical of the Twelve Apostles. In the same way, the trefoil in Gothic architecture is said to be symbolical of the Trinity; the quatrefoil, of the Four Evangelists, &c.; but it is foreign to our present purpose to go further into this part of the subject.

Melrose Abbey, the tourists' favourite, now claims exclusive attention. It was founded in 1136, and completed ten years later; but having been destroyed by Edward II. during his invasion in

1322, nothing of the original fabric remains. King Robert the Bruce—whose heart was destined to be deposited before the high altar here, instead of in the Holy Sepulchre at Jerusalem, as was his latest wish—granted a sum of £2000 towards its restoration. The work, which was carried on through the liberality of the king, was interrupted by the abbey being burned in 1385 by Richard II. of England, and most, if not all, the present building appears to have been erected subsequent to that date. In short, the Decorated style may be said to be taken up here just at the point where it leaves off at Jedburgh. Besides the centre alley and side aisles of the nave, there is a row of chapels along the south side; and in each of these chapels there seems to have been an altar, as indicated by the piscinæ that still remain. The exterior chapels, as seen here, are a feature more common on the Continent than in this country. They are, however, seen also in St Giles' Cathedral, Edinburgh, and in Elgin Cathedral. Contrary to the general rule, the north aisle is narrower than that on the south side. Rather more than half of the nave and of the side aisles has been destroyed; several of the chapels are now roofless; and of the tower—which was 84 feet in height—only the west side remains. The north transept is also roofless. There is no triforium, but simply a passage along the clerestory. In Jedburgh, as we have seen, the triforium is a principal feature; in Dryburgh, as has been pointed out, it is of small importance; and in Melrose it disappears altogether. All the roofs are of stone. The earlier builders contented themselves with arching the smaller aisles, but in later times they were possessed of more skill and confidence, and vaults were thrown over much larger spaces. On the south side of the nave double flying buttresses have been thrown over the chapels and aisle to resist the outward thrust of the principal roof, while the outer walls are supported by the usual shelving buttress, and all the buttresses are surmounted with pinnacles, so that their weight might render the building more stable and less likely to be overthrown. Innumerable niches with richly-carved canopies—many of them still containing statues—are seen throughout the edifice, and the numerous pinnacles, all panelled and

ornamented with crockets and other decorations, add greatly to the general effect. The windows display great variety of design, from the plain single light to those of one, two, three, and four mullions with elaborate tracery. Some of the tracery is geometrical, combined with that of a somewhat flowing character, all richly cusped; and the pear-shaped openings, like those in the small chapel window of Jedburgh, are of frequent occurrence. It may be noted that the window fifth from the transept on the south side of the nave is similar in design to the great north window in Jedburgh, but the former is much smaller. The only difference in the tracery is that at the top of the lower lights at Melrose there are double cusps, while in Jedburgh they are single. A circular window with rich tracery, in the north transept, is said to represent the "crown of thorns." The carver's art is seen here in perfection—roses, lilies, ferns, oak and ash leaves, curly greens, and "a thousand beautiful shapes besides, are chiselled with such inimitable truth and such grace of nature that the finest botanist in the world could not desire a better *hortus siccus*, as far as they go." A corbel in the north transept has been admired as a perfect gem. It represents a human hand holding a bunch of foliage, and supports one of the vaulting shafts. Lockhart, from whom we have just quoted, grew eloquent over this when he thus wrote in his *Peter's Letters to his Kinsfolk*:—
"Were it cut off and placed among the Elgin Marbles, it would be kissed by the *cognoscenti* as one of the finest of them all. Nothing could be simpler, more genuinely easy, more full of expression. It would shame the whole gallery of Boisserées." But it would seem that when the Romish clergy of the fifteenth century had become greatly corrupt, with only a semblance of sanctity, and when they were thought to be a fitting theme for the satirical poets, the sculptors connected with the Church did not hesitate to throw a little satire into its architecture. Hence we find, almost side by side with sacred texts and precepts, and angelic or saintly figures, representations of monstrous forms—monkish faces grinning irreverently, pigs playing on bagpipes, and other things not at all suited to a religious feeling.

Some writers have held that Melrose Abbey shows a mixture of all the styles from the Norman to the Perpendicular inclusive; but this is judging by English rules (which, even if strictly followed, would not bear out the supposition) a building entirely free from English influence. Previous to the War of Independence there was considerable intercourse between England and Scotland, but after that period everything English was disliked, and when aid of any kind was needed it was sought for from abroad rather than from the "auld enemies." Dr Daniel Wilson, the learned author of *The Archæology and Prehistoric Annals of Scotland*, devotes a chapter of that work to mediæval ecclesiology, in which he remarks, with much truth, that "for nearly a century the ecclesiastical architecture of England and Scotland is in one style, coincident in date and uniform in character of details;" but that "soon after the introduction of the First Pointed or Early English style a marked difference is discoverable, and therefore the dates and peculiar characteristics of the ecclesiastical architecture of the two countries disagree in many essential points." Again, while alluding to the Second Pointed or Decorated style, he says: "With the first symptoms of transition the ecclesiastical architecture of Scotland begins to assume its peculiar characteristic features, marked by a return to the use of the semicircular arch, and a preference of circular to angular details, employed, not indiscriminately or at random, but on a fixed principle, along with a consistent use of the pointed arch, and of details peculiar to the later styles." There was a mingling of the features of the First and Second Pointed, and from 1307, when Bruce ascended the throne, "the rules of English ecclesiology can only mislead the student of Scottish ecclesiastical architecture." It is well to bear these remarks in mind when examining the ruins of Melrose.

In the north transept there are two round-headed doorways, with the round bowtell moulding running up the jambs and round the arch; but there is no reason for believing that these are older than that leading from the north aisle to the cloister, which, with its characteristic base, roll and fillet moulding, and richly-carved capitals, bears unmistakable proofs of belonging to the Decorated period, though it also has the semicircular arch. This, it may be remembered, was the "steel-clenched postern" through which, according to the *Lay of the Last Minstrel*, the aged monk took Sir William Deloraine when on a visit to the grave of Michael Scott for the wizard's mysterious book. It should be observed that the foliage on the capitals of this doorway, as on all capitals of the Decorated period, has the appearance of being wreathed round the bell, instead of springing as it were from the neck-mould, as seen in the earlier styles. The foliage, as we have already said, has been copied from nature, and is not of that conventional kind seen in the Early English and Transition Norman periods.

Though the nave and transepts may be said all to belong to the Decorated period, we find here and there indications of a transition to the Perpendicular, which is more fully developed in and near to the chancel. The ogee-shaped canopy or hood, the counterpart of the depressed or four-centre arch, is seen in a recess in the cloisters, also over the south transept doorway and window, and over the great east window in the chancel. The arches underneath are of the usual pointed character; but over the recess and the doorway there is the characteristic square encasement ever suggestive of the latest style, and while the spandrels of the former are plain, those of the latter are filled with figures. It is well known that many of the Early Perpendicular doorways differed but little from those of the preceding period, the square encasement and ornament being all that distinguish them. The capitals and mouldings of the chancel show little or no change from those of the nave; and though the vaulting in the south transept has additional ribs, the same principle is observed as in the aisles. In the vaulting of the chancel, however, a new principle is introduced. The ribs get more into a sort of network, but very far from reaching to the fan-tracery vaulting, as seen in some parts of England, notably in that wonderful piece of workmanship, the roof of Henry VII.'s Chapel in Westminster Abbey. The bosses are elaborately carved; some have representations of foliage, others have human figures. One principal figure is seen bearing a crucifix; others with swords and staves. It is the windows specially, with their mullions going right up to the top, and their cusped transoms, that give unmistakable proofs here of the Perpendicular. The great east window is much admired, and Scott's description of it must be familiar to all:—

> "The moon on the east oriel shone
> Through slender shafts of shapely stone,
>   By foliaged tracery combined;
> Thou wouldst have thought some fairy hand
> 'Twixt poplars straight the osier wand
>   In many a freakish knot had twined,
> Then formed a spell when the work was done,
> And changed the willow wreaths to stone."

It has been admitted that, taken at best, no Gothic exterior can ever cope with the interior; so that when we see what richness in carving and exuberance of fancy have done for the outside of Melrose, we may well believe that the inside effect must have been grand indeed when the abbey was in its palmiest days. It must have been awe-inspiring to have stood under the high vaulted roof, to have looked along the "long-drawn aisles," to have seen the monks in the chapels saying mass for the repose of the souls of the departed, or to have gazed through the rood screen at the high altar with its rich furnishing at the far east, while the "dim religious light" shed its subdued rays on the clustered pillars, delicately-wrought capitals, and sacred images of the saints.

Little is known of the names of those to whose genius we owe the buildings of the abbeys of Teviotdale. They are lost, though their works partially remain. Theirs was a work of love and devotion to the Church, and they cared more for erecting temples for the worship of the Master than for rearing monuments for themselves.

THE END.

INDEX.

ABERNETHY, John, minister of Jedburgh, 107.
Abbotrule, barony and kirk of, belonged to Jedburgh Abbey, 57.
Abbots of Jedburgh. The abbot one of the king's magnates, 24; assisted in excommunicating the king's counsellors in Cambuskenneth Abbey, 25; safe conduct granted to the abbot by king of England, 25; law pleas with William of Bellingham, 26; the abbot one of three commissioners sent to Edward I. of England anent the rival claims of Bruce and Baliol, 32; attended meetings of the estates of Scotland, 32; Edward directs six fat bucks to be sent to the abbot, 33; was present when Baliol acknowledged Edward to be his feudal superior, 33; swore fealty to Edward I., 34; was one of the Scottish ambassadors to France in 1299, 36; attempt by the English king to intercept them at sea, 36; the abbots of Jedburgh not mitred abbots, 41. (For list of abbots, and particulars concerning each, see "Superiors of the Monastery," 72-80).
Abbotsley, church and advowson of, 38.
Aberlemno, kirk of, belonged to Restennot, 58.
Aidan, St, formed a church at Old Melrose, 169.
Ainslie, John, 139, 140.
Alexander III., married in Jedburgh Abbey, 28-30; his death, 30; disastrous effects, 31.
Ancrum, barony and kirk of, belonged to Jedburgh Abbey, 57.
—— interesting proceedings in the kirk of, 51, 52.

Ancrum Moor, battle of, 50.
Andrew, abbot of Jedburgh, 77.
Anthony, St, the founder of monachism, 2.
Arturet, patronage of the church of, 26.
Athanasius takes Egyptian monks to Rome, 3.
Aurchsook, lands of, granted to Jedburgh Abbey, 53.

"BEAUTEOUS ROSEBUD" of Burns, 143.
Bastenethwait, settlement of dispute anent advowson of the church of, 22.
Belses, barony of, belonged to Jedburgh Abbey, 57.
Benedict, St, the founder of Western monachism, 3.
Benedictines, chief agents in spreading Christianity and civilisation, 3.
Blackader, archbishop of Glasgow, probably helped to restore Jedburgh Abbey, 47.
—— Commendator of Jedburgh, 78.
Blair, Peter, minister of Jedburgh, 109.
Blantyre, abbot and convent of Jedburgh, patrons of, 58.
Boston, Rev. Thomas, 138, 139.
Bruce, King Robert the, granted a charter to Jedburgh Abbey, 52 and 163.
Buccleuch, Earl of, purchased from Sir John Ker the lands of Boxtonleys, Chiefthope, Over and Nether Whitkirk, and other lands which had belonged to Jedburgh Abbey; also the teinds of Castleton and Erkleton, and all other lands belonging to the old cell of Canonby, 63.
Burnett, James, minister of Jedburgh, 107.

INDEX.

CAMPBELL, Lord, 140.
Canonby, a dependency of Jedburgh Abbey, 57.
—— and Coldingham, erected into a barony and granted to the Earl of Home, 61.
Castleton, kirk of, belonged to Jedburgh Abbey, 57.
Charter, by Prince Henry, to the canons of Jedburgh, 159, 160.
—— by William the Lion, to the canons of Jedburgh, 160-162.
—— by Robert the Bruce, extract from the register of, granted by James IV., 163, 164.
—— confirming one of Andrew, commendator of Jedburgh, 164, 165.
Clayhillis, Andrew, minister of Jedburgh, 106.
Cranston, Thomas, abbot of Jedburgh, 77.
Creech, Peter, minister of Jedburgh, 106.
Cross, ancient, in Jedburgh Abbey, 128.
—— Anglo-Saxon, 127.

DALMENY, kirk of, belonged to Jedburgh Abbey, 57.
Daniel, prior of Jedburgh, 72.
David, Prince of Cumbria, founded Jedburgh Abbey and restored the fallen bishopric of Glasgow, 9; afterwards he became David I. of Scotland, 10; he was the "sair saunct," 169.
Decorated architecture in Dryburgh Abbey, 179.
—— —— in Jedburgh Abbey, 179, 180.
—— —— in Melrose Abbey, 180-184.
Ditch and hedge, earliest notice of, 26.
Douglas, John, minister of Jedburgh, 110.
—— William, of Bonjedward, helped in the reparation of Jedburgh Abbey after its destruction by the English in 1523, for which he received a grant of land, 48.
Donnyvald, kirk of, belonged to Restennot, 58.
Dryburgh, a religious house at, in the sixth century, 169.

Dryburgh Abbey, founded for Premonstratensian Canons, in twelfth century, 169.

EASTON, Robert, 144.
Early English architecture in Kelso Abbey, 178.
—— —— in Dryburgh Abbey, 178, 179.
Eckford, kirk of, belonged to Jedburgh Abbey, 57.
Ecgred, Bishop, gifted the two Gedworths to Lindisfarne, 7.

Forester, Andrew, minister of Jedburgh, 106.
Forfar, lands, &c., in, confirmed to the abbot and convent of Jedburgh, 32.
—— kirk of, belonged to Restennet, 58.

GALBREATH, William, minister of Jedburgh, 109.
Gedworth, first notice of, suggested meanings of the name. (See Jedburgh).
Grammar School of Jedburgh removed from the abbey in 1751, 93, 94.
Gysborne, Robert de, abbot of Jedburgh, 73.

HALL, John, abbot of Jedburgh, 43.
Hamilton, Sir Thomas, king's advocate, apprised the lands and lordship of Jedburgh from Sir John Ker, which was afterwards assigned to his son Thomas, Lord Binning, who led a new apprising against Sir John Ker, 64, 65.
Henry, abbot of Jedburgh, in 1239, 73.
—— —— in 1506, 78.
Hertford, Earl of, burned Jedburgh town and abbey in 1545, 50.
Hilson, Gavin, M.D., 142.
Hobkirk, kirk of, belonged to Jedburgh Abbey, 57.
Home, Andrew, commendator of Jedburgh, 79.
—— Earl of, excambed the lands and lordship of Jedburgh for the Hirsel, 62.

Home, John, abbot of Jedburgh, 78.
—— Lord, got lands and lordship of Jedburgh, 59.
—— Sir David, of Wedderburn, provided to the abbacy of Jedburgh, 64.
Hope, William, of Hope House, 143.
Hownam, kirk of, belonged to Jedburgh Abbey, 57.
Hume, Alexander, of Huttonhall, got the four mills of Jedburgh, 59.
—— William, minister of Jedburgh, 109.

JAMESON, William, minister of Jedburgh, 108, 109.
Jarum, William de, abbot of Jedburgh, 74-76.
Jedburgh, a royal burgh on the Jed, 7; first church at and character of the same, 8; town burned by the English in 1410, 1416, and 1464, 40; and in 1544 and 1545, 50; the burghers at Reidswire, 133; their slogan or war-cry, 133.
—— Abbey, extent of, 6; the monastery founded by David in 1118 for Canons Regular, 11; at first a priory and raised to an abbacy about 1147, 11; extent of the priory church and description of the work, 12-14; erection of the nave and extension of choir, with description of the work, 15-21; settlement of dispute between the bishop of Glasgow and the canons in 1220, 22, 23; royal marriage in, 28; a spectre appears at the dance, 31; documents deposited in the abbey ordered by Edward I. to be delivered over to Baliol, 33; abbey wrecked and plundered by the English, 35; prosperity of the abbey, 39; rebuilding of north transept, choir chapel, and tower, 39; description of the work, 39-47; abbey burned by the English in 1523, 1544, and 1545, 48, 49; suppression of the abbey at the Reformation, 55; possessions and revenues of, 146-150; rent roll, 151-155; spirituality of, 155-158.
Jedburgh Castle, abbot and convent of Jedburgh, along with Sir Ive Aldeburge, offered to undertake custody and repair of, 35; castle in the hands of English at time of Bannockburn, 37; taken by Sir James Douglas, 37; fell into hands of English after Battle of Neville's Cross, 40; demolished by the Scots in 1409, 40; difficulty of demolition, 40.
—— Robert, Lord, mortified a thousand merks for upholding the aisle of Ferniherst, 42; presented a bell to the kirk of Jedburgh, 90. (See also pp. 136, 137).
Jeffrey, Alexander, historian of Roxburghshire, 142, 143.
Jerdon, Archibald, 138.
John, abbot of Jedburgh in 1338, 76.
—— —— in 1390, 76.

KENNOCK, a doubtful personage, said to have been abbot of Jedburgh in the tenth century, 8.
Ker, Andrew, of Ferniherst, got grants for himself and heirs of the bailiary of the lands and lordship of Jedburgh Forest, 53. (See also p. 135).
—— Sir Andrew, of Hirsel, to appear at Justice Court at Jedburgh, 58.
—— Sir Andrew, of Ferniherst, confirmed in his office of bailiff of the lands and lordship of Jedburgh Forest, 60; created Baron Jedburgh in 1622, 64. (See also pp. 135, 136).
—— James, of Crailing and Hundalee, 136.
—— Sir John, of Ferniherst, 135.
—— Sir John, of Hirsel, got the mills of Jedburgh, which had belonged to the abbey, 62; excambed the lands of Hirsel for the lordship of Jedburgh, 62; had to find caution to settle the Laird of Ferniherst in his teinds in several parishes, 64.
—— Robert, of Crailing, 136.

INDEX.

Ker, Robert, son of Sir Andrew Ker of Ferniherst, contributed towards the restoration of Jedburgh Abbey, for which he got the lands of Ancrum-Woodhead, 48, 49.
—— Sir Thomas, 135.
Kelso, abbey of, built in twelfth century for Tironensian monks, 169.
Kentigern, St, altar in Jedburgh Abbey of, 67.

LESLIE, General the Hon. Alexander, 134.
Longnewton, kirk of, belonged to Jedburgh Abbey, 57.
Lothian, Earl of, purchased land and lordship of Jedburgh from the Earl of Haddington, 63.
—— Schomberg Henry, ninth marquis of, 103, 117; repairs Jedburgh Abbey at great expense, 117.
—— William Schomberg, eighth marquis of, 137.

MACKNIGHT, Rev. Dr, minister of Jedburgh, 110.
Magdalene, St Mary, hospital of, 38.
Margaret, the Virgin, bell of the Blessed, 99.
Mary, the Blessed, altar of, 68.
Masons' marks on Jedburgh Abbey, 122-124.
M'Kay, Daniel, minister of Jedburgh, 109.
Melrose, Old, church here in seventh century, 169.
—— Abbey, built for Cistercian monks in twelfth century, 169.
Methven, Paul, minister of Jedburgh, 105, 106.
Monachism, its early origin, 1.
Moden, St, formed church at Dryburgh, 169.
Monasteries, splendour of the, 3; their wealth, 55; description of them, and list of officers, 5; the vassals who worked on the land, 5, 6; number of monasteries suppressed in Scotland at Reformation, 55; number of persons officially connected with them, 55.
Morel, John, abbot of Jedburgh, 74.
Murray, Major John, 142.

Ninian, St, altar of, 69.
Nisbet, kirk of, belonged to Jedburgh Abbey, 57.
Norman, early, work in Jedburgh Abbey, 13, 14, and 170, 171.
—— Transition in Kelso Abbey, 172, 173.
—— —— Dryburgh Abbey, 173-175.
—— —— Jedburgh Abbey, 16-21, and 175-178.

OSBERT, abbot of Jedburgh, 73.
Oxnam, kirk of, belonged to Jedburgh Abbey, 57.

PACHOMIUS, formed the first regular cloister and nunnery, 2.
Panter, David, bishop of Ross, consecrated in Jedburgh Abbey Kirk, 54.
Paul, the first Christian hermit, 1.
Perpendicular work in Melrose Abbey, 184, 185.
Peter, abbot of Jedburgh, 73.
Philip, abbot of Jedburgh, 73.
Plenderleith, kirk of, belonged to Jedburgh Abbey, 57.
Popery, acts against papists and, 56, 57.
Prenderlathe, Nicholas de, abbot of Jedburgh, 73.
Preston of Pennycuik got pension from the abbacy of Jedburgh, 61.
Purves, Rev. Dr, minister of Jedburgh, 110.

RALPH, abbot of Jedburgh, 73.
Reformation, the, 55; number of conventual establishments suppressed in Scotland at, 55.
Reformed church in Jedburgh Abbey, at first under the tower, 82; decayed state of church and proposal to repair it with the timber of the refectory, 83, 84; Presbytery visitation, 85; John

Mill, a "maister of work," makes a report, 85, 86; removal from the tower to west end of nave, 90; removal from the abbey, 112-117; ministers of the reformed church, 105-111.
Religious reforms in twelfth century, 4.
Reperlaw, barony of, belonged to Jedburgh Abbey, 57.
Restennot, belonged to Jedburgh Abbey, 57; the priory, how situated, 58; erected into a barony in favour of Viscount Fentoun, 61.
Richard, abbot of Jedburgh Abbey, 72.
Riddell, Jean, 134.
Ritchie, Rev. Dr, minister of Jedburgh, 111.
Robert, abbot of Jedburgh in 1322, 76.
—— abbot in 1358, 76.
—— —— 1473, 77.
—— —— 1488, 77.
Roman altar, 128, 129.
Roof marks, double, on Jedburgh Abbey, 118-121.
Rowat, James, minister of Jedburgh, 110.
Rutherfurd, John, of Bankend, 133.
—— —— of Edgerston, 133.
—— —— of Mossburnford, 133.
—— of Fernington, 132.
—— of Fernilee, 132.
—— of Hundalee, 133.
—— of Hunthill, 133.
—— of the Hall, 132.
—— the Lorimer, 132.
—— Richard, of Littleheuch, 133.
—— Robert, of Todlaw, 51.
—— Robert, of Chatto, 131.
—— Thomas, slaughtered in monastery of Jedburgh, and remission for the same, 51.
—— William, of Longnewton, slaughtered in monastery of Jedburgh by Ker of Newhall, 51; happy result of the same, 52.

SEAL of the chapter of Jedburgh, 70, 71.
—— of Cardinal David Beaton, 132.

Selbie, kirk of, belonged to Canonby, 57.
Semple, Gabriel, minister of Jedburgh, 109.
Slogan or warcry of the men of Jedburgh, 133.
Shanks, Rev. Alexander, minister of Jedburgh, 144, 145.
Shortreed, Robert, 141, 142.
Somerville, Rev. Dr, minister of Jedburgh, 7, 137, 138.
Surrey, Earl, burned Jedburgh in 1523. 48; bears testimony to the bravery of the Borderers, 48.

THOMAS, abbot of Jedburgh, 77.
Thomson, Mungo, 144.
Turnbull, bishop of Glasgow, said to have helped to restore Jedburgh Abbey, 44.
—— David, of Wauchope, to appear at Justice Court at Jedburgh, 58.
Tynedale, William of, and other canons of Jedburgh exiled from Scotland because of their English origin, and petitions Edward III. of England for sustentation, 37.

ULSTON, barony of, belonged to Jedburgh Abbey, 6.
—— lands in, granted to Douglas of Bonjedward, for helping to repair Jedburgh Abbey, 48.

VEITCH, James, of Inchbonny, 144.

WALTER, abbot of Jedburgh, 77.
Warwick, the Earl of, burned Jedburgh in 1464, 40.
Wauchope, kirk of, belonged to Canonby, 57.
Winchester, James, minister of Jedburgh, 110.
Windington, barony of, belonged to Jedburgh Abbey, 57.
Winter, James, 141.

YOUNG, John, minister of Jedburgh, 106.

OPINIONS OF THE PRESS ON THE FIRST EDITION.

"Jedburgh Abbey has had the good fortune to find an historian of the right stamp, one who 'takes pleasure in her stones,' and who has carefully and lovingly constructed an interesting historical sketch of her fortunes out of scanty materials, patiently and laboriously collected, partly from printed books, but principally from unpublished documents. . . . . Mr Watson deserves credit for his patient research in the collection of materials, and for the arrangement of these materials into a readable and instructive narrative."—*Scotsman.*

"This brief account of Jedburgh may be said to contain the most of what we are ever likely to know regarding it, either from the historic or descriptive side. It is equally suited as a guide for strangers, or a handy reference book for those desiring to refresh the memory concerning events happening in or around the abbey."—*Glasgow Herald.*

"Mr Watson has gathered much information and many facts from a great variety of sources, and these have been woven into a well-sustained, interesting narrative. Jedburgh Abbey, without doubt, has found an historian of the first order."—*Kelso Mail.*

"This is just what an historical and descriptive handbook should be, namely, brief, clear, and everywhere to the point. The visitor to this interesting monument will find in Mr Watson an intelligent and useful guide, never saying more than is necessary, but always saying enough."—*Notes and Queries.*

"This is a work of considerable importance, whether we view it in the light of a contribution to current literature, or as helping towards a more perfect understanding of the most beautiful ecclesiastical ruin in the south of Scotland."—*John o' Groat's Journal.*

"As set forth in this volume the story is a wondrous and many-sided one, and the visitor to the old pile will find combined in Mr Watson's review voices from all ages, revealing, more or less fully, the character and conditions of life on the Jed for more than nine centuries. The work has been done carefully, the results are stated concisely but clearly, and without any great break of continuity. It is a fine story of Border life, addressed to Borderers, but also to reflective men all the world over."—*Daily Review.*

"Visitors will find Mr Watson's little handbook a most useful and instructive companion."—*Examiner.*

"Mr Watson has industriously gleaned from scattered sources the material for his book, and his narrative of the vicissitudes of the abbey is deeply interesting from its close connection with the religious history of the country."—*Edinburgh Courant.*

PRESS OPINIONS ON THE FIRST EDITION.

"Of its kind Mr Watson's work is a model of arrangement, condensation, and extensive information. . . . . It is also exceedingly well written, whether in the purely technical details of the architectural beauties of the venerable ruin, or in the description of the eventful and stirring scenes of which it has for centuries been the centre."—*Dundee Evening News.*

"Nothing could be better than the way in which the matter has been arranged, and the great difference between Mr Watson and an ordinary compiler is nowhere more clearly apparent than in the glimpses he gives his readers of the social life in which the ecclesiastical element bulked so largely. The entire volume affords a treat of no ordinary kind. . . . . It would be impossible to speak in too high terms of Mr Watson's architectural descriptions."—*Stirling Observer.*

"The materials for the work were somewhat scanty. . . . . All the more credit, therefore, is due to Mr Watson for having, by labour and research, succeeded in collecting so much data on the subject as his book discloses."—*Dumfries Standard.*

"His work has our heartiest recommendation, as one in which patient and extensive research has thrown its results into a very readable form."—*North British Daily Mail.*

"It is a piece of conscientious work which does the author great credit. Every page affords proof of patient investigation and successful research."—*Kelso Chronicle.*

"Altogether the work is singularly complete and exhaustive."—*Border Advertiser.*

"It is but scant justice to this little work to say that any future history of our noble abbey must of necessity be founded upon it, the information being fuller and more accurate than it can elsewhere be found, and put together in the most concise and attractive form."—*Teviotdale Record.*

"The book is one of rare excellence and much value, and will do more than any previous contribution of a like nature to give Jedburgh Abbey that prominence among the architectural remains of Scotland which it so well deserves."—*Jedburgh Gazette.*

"A valuable acquisition to Border historical and antiquarian literature. . . . . A description and history of the abbey, which, for its completeness and originality, is most unique."—*Hawick Advertiser.*

"I have to congratulate you on having completed your *Jedburgh Abbey* so successfully."—*Extract from letter from the late David Laing, LL.D., Signet Library, Edinburgh.*

www.ingramcontent.com/pod-product-compliance
Lightning Source LLC
Chambersburg PA
CBHW031744230426
43669CB00007B/477